Learn & Remember 25 Secret Hypnotic Language Patterns Now to Help You Become Rich

CHANGE MINDS, EARN MORE, WIN

Bryan Westra

Indirect Knowledge Limited
MURRAY, KENTUCKY

Bryan Westra/Indirect Knowledge Limited
2317 University Station
Murray, Kentucky/42071
www.indirectknowledge.com

Book Layout ©2014 IndirectKnowledge.com

Ordering Information:
Quantity sales. Special discounts are available on quantity purchases by corporations, associations, and others. For details, contact the "Special Sales Department" at the address above.

Learn & Remember 25 Hypnotic Language Patterns to Help You Become Rich/ Bryan Westra. —1st ed.
ISBN-10: 0990513211
ISBN-13: 978-0-9905132-1-6

Contents

Dedication to Jennifer Bonilla

If you see yourself as prosperous, you will be. If you see yourself as continually hard up, that is exactly what you will be.

—ROBERT COLLIER

Learn & Remember 25 Hypnotic Language Patterns to Help You Become Rich

Hi. My name is Bryan Westra. I'm an international hypnosis and NLP trainer. I love what I do. In this book, I'm going to concentrate on twenty-five specific hypnotic language patterns, you can learn to help yourself become financially prosperous—rich!

You're thinking, how can language, and hypnotic language at that, make me rich: And I have the answer to that question, which I'll share with you in a few moments time. You see, people are all the time going in and out of hypnosis. There's the well-known 'highway' hypnosis in which we're magically transported through space and time, incognizant of how we got to where we got. Sometimes we miss our exit and drive for miles, until finally we snap-to and realize we were in la-la-land, aware, and; yet, not aware. Other times we find ourselves unable to focus on our school work, or our professional work, and no matter how hard we try and focus, we simply can't.

Getting back to how language can make you rich, let me give you this to chew-on: Imagine yourself able to communicate with people, anyone for that matter, and be able to persuade them to take 'any' action you want them to take. I'm talking any action, now, mind you. If you want someone to buy something you have for sale, you would be able to simply ask them to buy it, and for the price you wanted to sell it, and credit card in hand, or better yet cash in hand, they'd be ready and willing to hand over their money to you. Or, let's pretend for a moment that you want to convince someone to drive you somewhere, perhaps on a long trip several hours away, and you want them to flit-the-bill for gas and snack along the way, and you simply sit back in the passenger seat, snacking on their snacks, and napping until you arrived. How would that make you feel: being in a position to do just that: influence and persuade anyone so that you could get what you wanted, anytime you wanted?

Before you answer that question to yourself, oops…you already have; but let me just finish here: You fall into two categories of people. One, when I asked you the previous question about how you'd feel, you thought: "Yeah…This would be amazing, and awesome. I'd love to be able to take advantage of somebody's charity, and have them sport-the-bill for me, and; yeah, that would be fantastic. Or, two, you fell into a category of people who instantly raised an objection flag to that type of scenario, because you felt uneasy taking advantage of somebody, and having them pay all the bills, and chauffer you around as if you're some king.

Now, regardless of which category you immediately found yourself in, let me just say it doesn't matter. The ability is what matters. There are many of you reading this, thinking: I would love to be more influential and persuasive, but I don't want to manipulate anybody, or take advantage of anyone. There are of you out there reading this who want, perhaps crave, the idea of controlling others with your persuasion skills. This book is written for anyone, and there's no judgment on anyone for what they want, what they think, or how they'll later use these language patterns.

You see the patterns themselves are not good or bad, helpful or evil; rather, they are simply words, which communicate ideas in a way that can help anybody, regardless of their intentions, hypnotize anybody through mere ordinary conversation. They make you more influential. They make you more persuasive. The get you what you want; regardless what it is you want. They are like a magic genie that serves only one purpose, which is to fulfill your wishes, nothing more, nothing less.

I am going to take you through some Ericksonian Language Patterns. So Milton Erickson was a legendary hypnotherapist in the United States and many of the patterns he used today not just in hypnotherapy but throughout, NLP and in many applications.

Before we begin, let's just talk about what the purpose is. What's the point of using these patterns?

The simple main purpose of using these patterns is to bypass conscious resistance. People's unconscious minds go much faster than their conscious minds. If you want to engage... then experiment with engaging at an unconscious level.

The other main purpose is to make what you are selling... (The ideas and concepts... the desired actions and outcomes... which you are aiming to persuade people to buy into...) to make them compelling, exciting, vivid and dynamic.

Now counter to what you might think consciously, few people are really persuaded by logical and rational arguments... especially not children who often lack the life experience upon which to buy into the basis of your apparently rational and logical arguments!

Ok, let's move on and talk a little bit about ethics and the ethical use of the Ericksonian Language Patterns.

Through-out this book I am going to take you through some of the key Ericksonian Language Patterns and there are lots of practical ways in which you can use these patterns to increase your capacity to influence and engage people in any context.

Please remember, however, that these patterns come from hypnosis originally and that Milton Erickson's intention was to help people not sell them things they don't really want.

I personally believe that our responsibilities towards other human beings still apply, whatever 'techniques' we choose to apply!

What this means is, stick to the same ethical guidelines that you are required to stick to within your profession. It also means, don't believe like an idiot! These patterns can be very powerful and beneficial when used in an honest and well-practiced manner, which places your client interest or your audience's interest at the heart of your practice.

However, if you attempt to use these patterns for personal gain, at other people's expense, you may or may not succeed in the short term but you will almost certainly find that you subsequently lose influence as people simply learn not to trust you.

So! Just stop for a moment and make a note of what you think the key ethical boundaries are for you in utilizing these powerful influencing tools within your professional context.

Now, I want to talk about well-formed outcomes. So what's the purpose of applying this particular language patterns? What are you hoping to achieve?

For these language patterns to enhance your influence in any situation you need to be working towards a well-formed outcome, a goal if you like.

So, for example, if you are a teacher, your well-formed outcome might be that your students enter into a vividly fantasized experience of what it was like to live during a certain period in time. Or it may be that you want them to actually complete their homework on time! It could really be anything you want to help them to learn.

If you are a leader in any context you may want your followers to really experience your vision for the future of your organization in all its sensory richness, imagining vividly all the benefits that will accrue to them personally (people tend to be self-motivated).

If you are in a career seeking to comfort someone in physical or mental pain, i.e. the helping profession, you may want to use these patterns to help someone distance themselves from their pain so that they can function more comfortably or maybe access a wider range of choices about their care.

Well-formed outcomes work best when they are stated positively, so you say what you want to happen; not what you don't want to happen.

A good well-formed outcome is also expressed in sensory terms... this means you think about what the outcome will look, sound, feel and even taste or smell like.

And although you are seeking to influence others, make sure that your well-formed outcome refers to you... that you own it. So, for example, you may want the students to finish that project on time, but your well-formed outcome will say something like, I will be so positive and motivated that students will find it almost impossible to resist my infectious enthusiasm and charisma.

Finally, do a quick check to ensure that what you are proposing to do fits well within the wider environment within which you are operating. So not only do you need to be clear about your ethical boundaries, but also to take real account of anyone else who might be affected by this outcome as you work towards it. In NLP, for those of you who have studied with me on a course or this blog, you'll know that this is called an Ecology check.

So once again, stop for a few moments and draft a simple, well-formed outcome within a professional context that you operate within.

Ok... so now we're ready to start practicing the Ericksonian patterns.

One of the most exciting and also sobering thoughts about these patterns comes from something Erickson himself once said: "Every word you use has the potential to have an effect now and twenty years from now."

Being precise is important when you're using these patterns and it is a good discipline to get into. At the same time, you want the patterns to flow naturally and to feel good as you use them.

The trick is practice, practice, practice. Some people like to write out these patterns; lots of different variations, lots of different examples of the same pattern, some people like to record themselves saying this patterns over and over. And the more you study these patterns, the more automatic the patterns will become. They become part of the way you naturally speak.

By listening and reaping these patterns and by accessing as many examples of people using these patterns you will, in your own time, begin to internalize and integrate these patterns into the way you influence others—in a way which seems natural and which is positive and ethical for you.

So let's begin with a pattern effect as Causal Links. These are links that combine a cause and an effect.

So setting up a chain of cause and effect, starting with statements which are verifiable and then gradually extending the cause effect statements into areas which you want your subjects to go along with even though these subsequence statements may not be actually verifiable.

So you're sitting here...

AND... You can feel the chair beneath you...

AND... It's twenty past three in the afternoon...

AND... You can hear my voice...

AND... You may also be aware of other sounds

AND... As you notice these sounds, no matter how slight...

You may also... begin to become aware... of how easy it would be... to *close your eyes right now*...

Using AND is the weakest form of casual link. It's one that no-one is likely to argue with. Once you have made a few statements using these 'AND' links you can progress, as in the example above, to the next level... and as you do so you may even notice the introduction of the word... 'as'... followed by the words... 'you may also'...

And as you begin to wonder what it would be like to close your eyes now...

As you continue to be vaguely aware of other sounds...

As you focus more and more on the sound of my voice...

As the clock ticks on...

Somehow... this makes you want to... just close your eyes...

so that you can image...

as you close your eyes now...

...imagine that you are...

...already...

developing the capacity to *see interactions* at a much smaller level...

at a molecular... even at a sub-atomic level...

and, as you begin to imagine what this might be like... to be able to...

And, of course, as you repeat each of these examples out loud...

so you may also... notice that each one makes you want to learn more. I hope you're getting the idea by now.

So words and phrases like 'makes' and 'persuades' and 'forces you to' ... all of these words are stronger than AND, AS YOU, and SO YOU MAY ALSO... so much so that what you will have noticed by now, I suspect, is that you start out simply stating facts and gradually increase the strength of your language as you shift effortlessly from what is true to what you want people to assume to be true...

So with causal links, you start where the subjects are, your obvious facts, and then you lead you subjects where you want them to go... in NLP, you will remember, assuming you have any knowledge of NLP, we call this PACING and LEADING... but I'm sure you knew that didn't you?

In fact, you can do this to such an extent that even where the starting point is negative... say the students are disengaged in a classroom...

You pace their level of disengagement... and then you gradually begin to lead...

Ok students... I know that some of you are not yet fully engaged with this topic... AND... I also know that you want to enjoy yourselves whilst you are here... AND as you sit here... AND as you listen to me talking... so much so that if you want to close your eyes... just for a few moments... and begin to imagine... what it is going to make you feel like... when you begin to feel so much more involved... when you find a new way of making this more interesting... more exciting... more relevant...

So write out the causal links you can spot in that last sequence now... then we'll move onto a couple of other patterns using 'awareness predicates' and maybe even a little 'mind reading'.

Awareness Predicates

Let's start with a list of these awareness predicates. I have put these into a set of phrases (some of these use additional patterns that we will be referring to later).

An awareness predicate is something, a word which basically indicates that you have some knowledge, some consciousness, some awareness, and some memory; that is, some *fantasy* about a particular topic or issue or subject. So, here is a list of awareness predicates to help you, as you communicate hypnotically-persuasive with the language patterns you'll be learning how to quickly remember in this book:

- I know...
- You may be aware...
- You can even do it using a negative
- I don't know to what extent...
- As you begin to remember...
- Perhaps you can imagine...
- As you may have considered...
- So too you can think about...
- However much you are already exploring...

So you get the idea. All of this word in some way or another refer to the process of being aware of being conscious of and being one way or another.

So the actual words you might have rationalized already are:

- Know
- Aware
- Don't know
- Remember
- Imagine
- Considered
- Think
- Explore

It is also worth noting that most words that begin with —*re* are hypnotic in nature and can help you send your subject's into a deep hypnotic state.

In fact any word which implies some kind of conscious or semi-conscious, cognitive processing... although of course, you may already be processing all of these patterns at a much less conscious level... I wouldn't know to what extents you are already experimenting with these patterns... perhaps even outside of your own conscious awareness... if you can imagine doing that right now?

One other thing you may have noticed... is that as you think about these patterns... whether I say you may have spotted... or your many NOT yet be aware that... either way, I am encouraging you to think and I'm drawing your attention to whatever follows the awareness predicate because your unconscious mind does not recognize negatives... is liable to lead you to do so right away... isn't it.

Awareness predicates... and the phrases they are embedded in are incredibly useful because... they tend to just lead you into additional forms of artful vagueness... influencing patterns... which help you to simply get into the flow of using Ericksonian language patterns... without too much conscious effort... if you can imagine that?

So now that you have explored casual links and awareness predicates you may also begin to spot some of the other patterns that I am using... almost coincidentally... I mean, I wouldn't want to 'presuppose' this is already happening... or would I? Tell you what... just because we can... let's have a *think about* 'presuppositions' and also *mind reading...*

Mind reading is simply the most direct way of using awareness predicates... I KNOW that... This is one example of you mind reading which I KNOW you'll understand immediately after reading this, now.

You KNOW what your subject is going to say... You can GUESS what is going to happen this instant... and these are examples of encouraging mind reading in others. It is interesting when you do this, how willing and compliant someone (your subject) is to follow your insistence that they do know something; namely, because you know they don't really know.

In a sense you simply presuppose what is going to happen next, or what you subjects are going to focus on now.

Let's go into presuppositions in more depth now, shall we? Presuppositions are incredibly useful when you use them in sequences where you stack one presuppositions on top of another. Just using one, however, might make your subject raise a red resistance flag, and this could instantly break all rapport that had been established. So you want to stack presuppositions, so that your subject just assumes, without effort or objection, what you are claiming or presupposing is in point of fact—the truth!

It is actually very difficult to say anything without using a presupposition. I am presupposing right now that you know what it means to 'say' something and also that you know what a 'presupposition' is, and for this reason you'll appreciate that you already know how to talk hypnotically even more than you know. There I go again, using a mind-reading pattern, as well as a presupposition; that is to say, I'm assuming for you that you know more than you think you know, and…well…how would I really know that, considering I have never likely met you.

So when you become really adept at influencing and engaging others it will in part be due to your very deliberate and artful use of presuppositions. It's hard not to use a presupposition…dang…did it again.

I don't know how many presuppositions can you spot in that particular sentence?

It's also very powerful to stack presuppositions one on top of another… and you'll know how to do this already at some level… I don't know how you know how to… somehow… whether it is now or in a few moments' time… consciously or unconsciously… before you started to think about this… or once you have considered it for a while… once you have practiced spotting… and using presuppositions… perhaps after you have completed the homework… or even as you do the homework now…

So see how many you can dig out from that one if you like.

In fact there are so many ways to presuppose… that when you start to presuppose the successful outcomes which I know you have already begun to think about… for your target audience… for your group of subjects… it's just a matter of time… or perhaps a matter of giving the appearance or illusion of choice… because whichever way you think about this now… consciously and deliberately… or at a more intuitive and less conscious level… either way… you are going to think… and act upon… all of these ideas… sooner… or later… whether you do it my way… or another way… whatever way it is going to work for you.

I'll let you spot all the presuppositions from now on... so you can relax, whether you have got it yet... or you are still practicing... either way... etc. etc. etc.

So let's now move on to a very important aspect of the way in which you use these language patterns. So not so much with the language pattern, rather how you say the language patterns that you are actually imploring.

Let's call it 'tonal marking' for now... although you will spot that there are other ways of marking out key words and phrases other than with the tone of your voice... by the time we are done... like the pace, for example, or the pitch... whether your intonation goes down at the end of the sentence... or up... for example... even how you use your hands, the angle of your head... and many, many other ways... the art is to 'punctuate' the word or phrase in such a way as to draw attention to it... at least, to draw attention at a less than obviously consciously level... if you can make sense of that?

I mean if you want to turn a phrase into an embedded command... all you need to do is to mark out the phrase... the suggestion... the embedded command... tonally... and simply *drop your voice*... at the end of the phrase...and this will tonally mark out the embedded command so it imprints on your subject's hypnotic mind (unconscious mind).

For more examples of tonal and analogue marking and for information on embedding commands and suggestions let's turn to get into the actual language patterns I'll be teaching you from this point out, shall we?

Oh, by the way, you'll know by the end of this book, how all these mysterious learnings I've just given you, work to create those well-formed outcomes I talked about—the results you're seeking, which will—make you rich beyond wonder!

CHAPTER 1

Hypnotic Communication Foundations: What You Need To Know To Successfully Use Hypnotic Language Patterns

The language patterns you'll be learning and mastering re-membering in the forthcoming chapters will help you be a much more hypnotic communicator. You may be new to hypnotic language and communication, and if so, that's fine, because I'm going to take a this chapter to catch you up to speed on what you need to know, before you start learning the 25 hypnotic language patterns.

You see communicating hypnotically is a skill they don't teach you in school. As such, many people, when they do find out about this covert form of communication, wonder if they really need it or not. This is a valid thought to have, considering that if you haven't learnt these skills by now in life, and have managed to get along just fine, then why bother taking the time to learn them now.

Why Learn How to Speak Hypnotically

When you look around you, and think about all the people in power; you know, the people you see on the news, the heads of state, and heads of Fortune companies. The rich people, or the people in power, that's who these people are. After you finish reading this book, have learnt these language patterns, and are fully abreast of this knowledge, and how to apply it, and use it for your own gain, you'll begin to assess how other people communicate, and be astonished to learn that the world's leaders are actually some of the best communicators. Some of them, and you'll quickly learn who they are, if you pay attention, are hypnotic communicators.

When you learn how to communicate hypnotically, using these hypnotic language patterns, you'll be able to build indestructible rapport with other people, to the extent you are able to get what you want from them. If you can get what you want from other people, without effort of force, or twisting their arm, then you can be just as powerful as these heads of states and the most powerful people on the planet.

I want you to suspend your disbelief, you know, your doubts, about what learning these 25 hypnotic language patterns will do for you. This is critical, because any time in my life where I have suspended my disbelief and doubts about something presented to me; especially, when it sounded too good to be true, I always benefitted. Other people I personally know, have told me the same thing. And think about it: If you don't suspend your doubts you never fully live. Had you (assuming you are happily married) not suspended your doubts about marriage and commitment, particularly in a world where divorce is so rampant, you'd never have married the person you love. Had you not suspended your doubts about learning how to swim, knowing many people drown each and every year, who have learnt to swim, you may have never experienced the pleasure of swimming. Had you bought into your doubts about driving, you may never have experienced the thrill of driving, even given the fact that many fatal accidents happen every year.

You see by suspending your disbeliefs and taking a leap of faith you get to experience and learn new things that possibly have a powerful impact on your life, and which may leave a powerful imprint on your memory.

This is why I ask you to suspend your disbelief for a short while, as you read this book, study these language patterns, and do the exercises. If you can do this, my promise to you is that you'll benefit yourself in an astonishing way, which leaves you feeling feelings of wonderment and empowerment that will help you to stay in power and control of your life for the rest of your life.

Hypnotic language patterns are only one element to speaking and conversing hypnotically. You must have a basic understanding of how to use these hypnotic language patterns, and some other aspects of hypnotic language—for example, you need to understand how to use your voice hypnotically, how to create a hypnotic rhythm to your words, how to stare at someone so they begin falling into hypnosis, and, most importantly, how to know when someone is hypnotized.

For this reason, I'm taking this chapter to explain all these basic principles to you. You might want to think of this chapter as a short course is conversational hypnosis. Of course, I haven't intentioned this book being a book on conversational hypnosis, as much as I have intentioned it more for learning 25 very powerful hypnotic language patterns. If you're needing or wanting to know more about conversational hypnosis or sales hypnosis then feel free to visit www.indirectknowledge.com as I have authored books, courses, and flashcards, that are exhaustive on the subject, and will greater assist you.

Imagine selling (we all sell everyday our ideas if not products and services) and closing the deal to get what you want by helping other people get what they want without failure. Consider how much more influential you'll be once you master these 25 hypnotic language patterns, knowing you'll be able to have other people believing your persuasions. By the time you finish this book, you'll be a great farther ahead of most people who haven't learned to master hypnotic language communication—that's my promise to you.

What You Need to Know Now About Communicating Hypnotically

Okay, I mentioned in the previous section that you need to have some foundation in conversational hypnosis in order to know how to apply the upcoming 25 hypnotic language patterns. In this section, I want to cover that material, and in the next section give you some instruction on how to take what you learn here and apply it usefully, so that when the time comes to learn the 25 hypnotic language patterns you'll be able to meaningfully put into action the patterns, and learn them much faster.

Embedded Commands

Embedded commands are short suggestions that are nested in phrases and sentences covertly which when analogue marked get picked up by the hypnotic mind, but not by the conscious mind. The hypnotic mind, incidentally, is what most people refer to as the subconscious mind or unconscious mind. This mind is responsible for all of our autonomic processes, which are unconscious to us most of the time—for example, breathing is something we do without thinking about, as well as our heart beating. We don't have to intentionally think about causing ourselves to breathe any more than we have to think about driving, once we learn it. So driving is another subconscious act. Basically, once we learn something, and learn it so well that we can do it without thinking about it, our learning becomes accomplished by our hypnotic mind, i.e.

our actions become hypnotic. This is why I call it the 'hypnotic mind'.

Embedded commands could be something like 'buy this now' and when placed in a sentence like: So many people are able to 'buy this now' and enjoy the beauty that comes with owning it. You see how I've analogue marked this sentence with single quotation marks. This is rather obvious, but when you are speaking an embedded command you can do the same thing, only more subtly, simply by pausing for a couple seconds before and after speaking this embedded command.

What happens is the hypnotic mind will process this command, much like a subliminal message, and carry out the action hypnotically without your realizing the suggestion wasn't your idea.

Sometimes hypnotists refer to embedded commands are 'hypnotic sentence fragments', so don't be confused if you hear them mentioned by this term. The more common and colloquial term is 'embedded commands'.

Analogue marking can be done in a number of ways. For example you can look into someone's left eye when you speak the embedded command, as their left-eye is connected to the right hemisphere of their brain, which is responsible for creativity and emotion, but also the hypnotic mind.

You can also click a clicker pen, while delivering the embedded command, or make a snapping noise before and after the command, to mark it out. Basically, you can do anything really that marks out the command, and the hypnotic mind will pick up on it, while the conscious mind will not.

Hypnotic Voice

Sometimes people think that a low deep voice is the best means for hypnotizing someone; however, this approach may not work so well in covert communication contexts, as it makes you seem strange, and would be rather out of context, incongruent, and in stark contrast too dramatically different than your normal conversation voice. For this reason it would likely raise some red flags and people would be on guard to what you were up to.

In my opinion the best hypnotic voice is subtle slowing down, gradually, in which you slow down to 1/3 your normal rate of speed, while also transitioning into a monotone. Think the boring college professor who has recited the same lesson lecture over and over, year after year, to every new freshman class, to the point where he or she is bored of delivering the content, and now speaks in a monotone and slow enough to let the students take his/her notes. There isn't a lot of passion in his/her voice. It's a monotone that causes the student to want to fall asleep, or begin daydreaming about something unrelated.

I think the monotone works best because it is very inconspicuous, yet also very hypnotic. You can say a lot of things that will not be picked up by someone, simply because they find it challenging to pay attention to everything you're saying, and for this reason you're able to state embedded commands easily without your subject's critical thinking faculty becoming alert to what you're actually delivering to the individual.

Hypnotic Repetition

Perhaps nothing is more hypnotic than repetition. It is in my opinion one of the reasons why in school teachers insist that their students 'repeat', 'repeat', 'repeat' their math problems, and spelling word lists. We learn facts and information by repeating it over and over until it becomes picked up by the hypnotic mind. Repetition in and of itself is very hypnotic.

One of the training aids we have developed at indirectknowledge.com are multiple flashcard decks for this very reason. They help the student of hypnosis to master hypnotic language at an accelerated rate, and in a way that is entirely a hypnotic experience. We'll be creating some flashcards using index cards later in future chapters to aid you in learning these 25 hypnotic language patterns faster and easier.

Music is very repetitious, having consistent beats that can be measured using a metronome —and, so, music too is very hypnotic. The humming sound of a refrigerator, or tires on a highway can also be very hypnosis inducing.

Your voice cadence can be adjusted to make what you say extremely hypnotic.

Signs of Hypnotic Trance

When someone is becoming hypnotized they exhibit certain physical characteristics—for example, their breathing will start to slow down, their pulse rate will slow, their physiology starts to calm down, their facial muscles start to soften and relax, their eye pupils will enlarge (dilate), and they will usually become much more agreeable and less in conflict with your suggestions. They simply take on the demeanor of a mindless sleepwalker and can be more easily manipulated, persuaded, indoctrinated, and made to agree with and act on certain suggestions—even suggestions they might under normal conditions, but even duress—never act on.

How to Communicate Hypnotically

Now that you know why it is important to communicate hypnotically, and what you need to know to be able to communicate hypnotically, I want to help you integrate all of these points, and teach you 'how' to exactly communicate hypnotically so that you can literally hypnotize anyone by having a simple, non-threatening, conversation with them. Learning this is something that great politicians have done and used to accomplish winning national elections, while also creating goodwill for their personal brand—ensuring a successful and longstanding political career. You can do the same, only applying it for your own particular purposes. If you want to sell more, you can. If you want to have greater control over those you manage, you can. If you want to compel someone to do your bidding for you, you can. So now let's learn how.

To start with you need to have a holistic wide-view of all the points I mentioned concerning: (a) embedded commands or hypnotic sentence fragments, (b) hypnotic voice, (c) hypnotic repetition, and (d) hypnotic trance signs. If you can keep these four critical concepts in your mind, you can hypnotize anyone without effort.

However, we need to synthesize this down a bit, and make it a process. A process is synonymous with action. Often times, linguistically, when we communicate ideas we do so in concrete terms. These are known to linguists as 'nominalizations' and these are verbs, adverbs, and even adjectives, which have been turned into nouns. A noun, if you recall back to the days of elementary grammar classes, is a 'person', 'place' or 'thing/object'. The word 'process' is a noun, which is also a nominalization; namely, one that has come about from the infinitive verb, 'to proceed'. Proceeding means moving forward and taking action. The word 'action' is another noun which has been nominalized from the infinitive verb, 'to act'. In order to 'proceed' or 'act' we should have a process map to help us take the necessary steps to complete a goal and gain a desired result.

The process map shows us how to do something. In the case of how to hypnotically communicate these are the steps of our process map:

I. Begin by talking to someone in a normal tone of voice, at a normal rate of speed, in a usual manner.

II. Learn to listen, and be slow to speak. In place of speaking, ask questions when appropriate, and use verbal pauses and attention words (e.g., Mmm, Sure, Right, I see, Okay, Yes, etc.) to build rapport, and to help you prove to your hypnotic subject, you are paying attention to them. This is important because the first step to hypnotizing someone is to gain their full attention, and if you are paying full attention to them, then you can be sure that they are paying attention to you fully, as well.

III. Start to slow down your speaking and lower your voice slightly. Make this a subtle shift that gradually shifts to 1/3 the rate of speed you began talking to them in. When you slow down, they will start to slow down too, and in the process start to fall under the spell of hypnosis.

IV. Start to repeat ideas and hypnotic suggestions, i.e. embedded commands; marking them out with either gestures, or short pauses before and after the delivery of the embedded command.

V. All the time while you are doing these above steps, be on the lookout for signs of hypnotic trance happening. You'll notice as your subject begins to slow down their speech, mirroring your slower rate of speed, that their physiology will also start to slow down, and that they'll start to enter trance. You'll see their facial muscles soften, you'll see their eyes dilate, you'll see their breathing slow, you'll see their focus on you strengthen and improve on you. They'll start to blank out, and begin agreeing with your ideas without questioning your authority or statements. In a sense they'll become putty in your hands, and you'll be able to mold them and control them as you like.

So this is 'how' we take the concepts I've shared before, and, turn them into a process for quickly and easily hypnotizing anybody, anytime, anywhere, as you like—just like that. It is a quick process, and it requires your full attention on them, to determine when they're hypnotized and when they're not. This is very similar to the process one might employ when they learn that their boss is upset and angry. You'd let them calm down, gather their thoughts, and then start to communicate your ideas with them, knowing that they're much more receptive in this calmer, hypnotic state. It's all psychology, and it works brilliantly, so start practicing this hypnotic process immediately, and constantly, until it becomes second nature for you.

How Else You Might Want To Use This Knowledge Of Hypnotic Communication To Benefit Yourself And Others

When you're working things out in your mind, and you're learning something new, like how to communicate hypnotically, it is important to consider all the various applications that this knowledge might server you usefully.

When I first began learning about conversational hypnosis, it was strictly to allow me to carryon on my sales career. At the time I wasn't batting a hundred, if you know what I mean.

I needed money in a bad sort of way. I was fixing to lose everything I had (which wasn't much looking back on the situation). Anyway, I absorbed this information like a sponge soaking up spilt milk. I wasn't going to cry about my situation, but I was certainly concerned about how I was going to pay the bills each month, keep a roof over my head, and keep food in my stomach.

What I did was start learning applying what I learned and instantly I started to see results improve. One day I earned in a day, what most people can hope to earn in a year. That was an amazing experience, which brought with it feelings of astonishment, and incredible gratefulness. It was a 'high' I'll never forget, because it was in that moment I realized I'd never want for anything, nor have to worry about my finances ever again.

What I didn't realize, which I want you to realize, is that there's a lot of possibilities: You can use conversational hypnosis to influence outcomes in situations that aren't sales related, necessarily. You can use them in your preaching ministry, if you happen to be a preacher or minister. You can use them to get a raise, or; for that matter, use them to get the dream job you've always wanted.

A few hours ago, I took a trip 45 minutes away, to give myself a break from writing, and peruse a bookstore. One of the books I observed, was by Robert Kiyosaki, with the title: *Why "A" Students Work for "C" Students and Why "B"*

Students Work for the Government. The idea was that 'C' students are more creative, less concerned with memorizing facts and figures, and tend to use their brains more to apply their creativity applicably, and for this reason make great entrepreneurs. The 'A' student tends to find a job, doing what is expected of them; finding themselves working for the entrepreneurs of the world.

I want you to know that you're only limited by your thinking. If you will take time out to do some thinking about how you can apply these lessons; explicitly, the hypnotic language patterns, yet, also, the foundational material we covered in this chapter on conversational hypnosis protocol, you'll be able to not only make a lot of money using these lessons, you'll also be able to have a lot of fun, and enjoy a rich and rewarding lifestyle.

Final Purport

In this chapter you discovered the foundations of hypnotic communication, in order to know what to do, and how to use, the forthcoming hypnotic language patterns I'll be teaching you. You learned about the power of using your voice; namely, the hypnotic monotone and hypnotic wav dynamics. You also learned the importance of paying attention, wholeheartedly, to your hypnotic subject, so that you can determine when they have fallen under the spell of hypnosis, and when they aren't. You learned about embedded commands in brief, which are also called hypnotic language fragments. You also learned about the importance of voice tonality and rhythm. All in all, you learned a lot, and what you've learned up to now, will greatly assist you in the future when you actually start to use the 25 hypnotic language patterns to affect people's emotional states, behaviors, and help them swing over to your persuasions, as you indoctrinate them and educate them in everything important to you.

Action Steps

There is a principle someone taught me once, which they labeled the 'Law of Action'. It basically claims, that you can learn anything, be the most brilliant mind, but if you don't take what you know and put it into action, it's worthless. I'm guilty of this, so let me be first to raise my own hand.

For years I learned information from reading books, attending seminars, being a student (I have multiple degrees), and still I remained broke, and sometimes penniless.

Then I read a book, and got inspired to take action, and start sharing all this knowledge with others. I took a job as a sales trainer, and taught others what I knew, and not surprisingly the company I contracted to prospered abundantly. Then I started my own company, and began experiencing huge results. Today, I have a new habit: I take what I learn and teach it to others, for profit of course, and I love it. Action is my best friend, and was the missing ingredient in my life. Since I learned this law, I have never looked back, and my life has become a lot more meaningful, and more richly rewarded.

All of this being said, I encourage you to do the following action steps; not because I want to waste your time, but because I want you to have the results you want. You should maximize the value of this book, and earn an exponential return on your investment, my opinion anyway!

I. Practice conversing with other people, anyone; it doesn't matter who, and begin using your voice hypnotically, to drop them into trance and under the spell of hypnosis.

II. Create some embedded commands, i.e. hypnotic sentence fragments, and begin slipping them into your conversations using the technique of 'analogue marking'.

III. Think about ways you can use this foundational material. It could be that you want to win more friends, make yourself more likeable, and just be a better communicator in general, but think about this for some time and come up with a few on your own.

CHAPTER 2

Powerful Hypnotic Language Patterns That Hypnotize

This chapter delves into the mysterious world of hypnotic language. It covers why you need to know the language patterns in this book. It provides you with a general overview of what you need to know about hypnotic language patterns. It will give you the fundamentals on how to use hypnotic language patterns effectively. I will also be exploring how else you might want to consider using these language patterns, while giving you opportunity to explore on your own some other contexts where using hypnotic language patterns might be useful for you. This chapter, more than anything, introduces you to one aspect of indirect, covert, conversational hypnosis; namely, hypnotic language. By learning these patterns, you can seamlessly, without thinking much about it, always have the 'right' thing to say, when you need it most.

Why Are Hypnotic Language Patterns Important For You To Learn

Some people have trouble accepting just how powerful hypnotic language patterns really are. What in the world does hypnosis and hypnotic language patterns have to do with captivating your audience? The answer is: Everything! Imagine the feeling of being able to hold the attention of everyone you're speaking to or presenting to, whether it is one on one in front of thousands. The fact is, unless you can keep all eyes and ears riveted on you while you're presenting, your message will be watered down at best, and what you want, you won't likely get.

What You Need To Know About This Hypnotic Language Pattern

Hypnotic language patterns came out of the studies of hypnosis, psychology and sales. When language patterns were first discovered the psychotherapy community realized that they could be used inappropriately.

Also using hypnotic language pattern can help you making more successful sales calls. You do this by reframing an experience or desire for a product, to by making the client feel more positive about the product. It guides the client to subconsciously or hypnotically agree and feel good about buying the product or service from you. It is the difference between being turned away and making the sale.

How To Use Hypnotic Language Patterns To Effectively Win People Over To Your Persuasions

Using powerful persuasion techniques in everyday life is what this book is primarily about. Amazing results can be achieved through the use of hypnotic language patterns. They are simple to use; yet, very powerful tools — and, you will want to add them to your skills as soon as you see the power through your experiences using them in real life applications.

Hypnosis and hypnotic language however, might be utilized to sidestep the safety that is frequently intrinsic when asking immediate inquiries. If for example, you ask, "How many of you here ran a red light recently?" This may cause some nervousness among the audience members. By changing the way you "ask" that question, they won't even know a question has been asked. If you say, "Now, I don't know how many of you have run a red light recently...." Let's examine what happens when it's "asked in this manner.

The listeners mind will access the exact same thing. Think of it like this; if you ask the question directly, they'll think about whether they have run a light or not. Using the hidden question also causes them to think the very same thing, with one huge difference; they feel as though they decided to think about it when you use the power of hidden questions.

How Else This Hypnotic Language Pattern Might Be Utilized Applicably In Other Useful Contexts

The embedded command is a preferred language pattern for many and you will see yourself time and time again cheerfully sliding these in and out of your language while getting closer to that increasingly achievable goal.

To begin with—do not try to embed more than five words when delivering an embedded command. There's no research which supports that shorter commands are more effective; however, using a bit of common sense will demonstrate to you that in everyday life the commands we give to others are often short and concise. And this leads us on to the essence of embedded commands and hypnosis in general; the exploitation of learned associations. While you're pondering this you may realize that the purpose of an embedded command is to articulate something in such a way that it triggers the same emotional anchor/association that is linked to everyday commands; done to prime predictable behavior, and ensure obedience.

Final Purport

In summary, these hypnotic language patterns can be used in various ways to benefit you in your daily life, as we have discussed in this chapter. These language patterns are useful in increasing your sales, in helping you to persuade other people to take to your ideas, and also they can help you win over the heart of another.

Furthermore, you'll find that when you learn the forthcoming hypnotic language patterns that you'll soon discover their efficacy, and wonder why you were never taught them in your interpersonal communication and public speaking courses in college or high school. These patterns are worth their weight in gold, because they essentially give you the Midas touch. You can equate these patterns with never having to be broke, since you can always use them to help you sell anything, and quickly, and for more money than you would otherwise be able to command elsewise.

Embedded commands or what is also known in hypnosis circles as 'hypnotic sentence fragments' are a powerfully covert means of communicating directly with someone's hypnotic mind or what most people refer to as the subconscious or unconscious mind. Delivering direct commands, through indirect hypnotic language patterns, means you'll master the artfully vague hypnotic language patterns in order to effectively bring down the guard of resistance someone has built around themselves to protect their well-being and self-interests, while also getting them to do what you want them to. This is remarkable, and you'll know what I mean, as you learn more and more of these hypnotic language patterns.

Action Steps

There is a principle someone taught me once, which they labeled the 'Law of Action'. It basically claims, that you can learn anything, be the most brilliant mind, but if you don't take what you know and put it into action, it's worthless. I'm guilty of this, so let me be first to raise my own hand.

For years I learned information from reading books, attending seminars, being a student (I have multiple degrees), and still I remained broke, and sometimes penniless.

Then I read a book, and got inspired to take action, and start sharing all this knowledge with others. I took a job as a sales trainer, and taught others what I knew, and not surprisingly the company I contracted to prospered abundantly. Then I started my own company, and began experiencing huge results. Today, I have a new habit: I take what I learn and teach it to others, for profit of course, and I love it. Action is my best friend, and was the missing ingredient in my life. Since I learned this law, I have never looked back, and my life has become a lot more meaningful, and more richly rewarded.

All of this being said, I encourage you to do the following action steps; not because I want to waste your time, but because I want you to have the results you want. You should maximize the value of this book, and earn an exponential return on your investment, my opinion anyway!

I.   Decide what you want from someone and experiment freestyle with asking various questions of the person to see if they'll 'give in' and give you what you want. Pay particular attention to how you ask the questions, what questions you ask, and your subject's physiology.

When you find what works, repeat this with someone new, and continue testing. At some point you'll have an experience that you can calibrate which will work more often than not. You need these types of experiences, because as a student of hypnotic language, you need to be well aware of how people respond, as well as what works and what doesn't work, yet more importantly 'why' it works.

II.   Make your communication more interesting by being genuinely interested in the people you communicate with from now on. Your sincerity and authenticity, will ensure you communicate with less resistance, as your subject's hypnotic mind can pick up on your interest or lack thereof; regardless, of how well you think you can 'fake' being interested or not. Make it a point to align yourself with authentic values and always be interesting to others. Note the results, mentally or on paper—you'll be shocked by what happens when you comply with this action step.

CHAPTER 3

Hypnotic Language Pattern One of Twenty-Five

HYPNOTIC LANGUAGE PATTERN:

THE MORE ___, THE MORE ___

When listening to famous public speakers, almost every-one starts to wonder how these people manage to deliver the speeches that not only captivate everyone's attention, but also moves people to take actions immediately. These questions inspire linguists to examine closely these speeches and discover some unique hypnotic language patterns effective speakers used in their art of persuasion. One of the most simple yet powerful hypnotic language patterns is the structure 'The more___ the more___'. The beauty of this pattern is that the more you learn about it and understand it, the more you realize how effective and powerful it is to help you achieve your goals.

In this chapter I'm going to be sharing with you an amazing hypnotic language pattern that is going to help you in your day to day language use due to its flexibility and its strength on application. First, I'm going to share with you 'why' this is important, and talks about how you can use it often and in almost application scenario. Then I'm going to be sharing with you 'what' you need to know about this particular 'hypnotic language pattern', specifically covering the "the more.... the more..." Next I'm going to literally explain to you 'how' you can use this hypnotic language pattern to achieve some persuasion impact on the person being addressed and giving yourself some room to convince an individual. Finally, I'm going to explore with you some other ways this hypnotic language pattern might actually help you indirectly do a better presenting your persuasions orally and in writing.

Why Is This Hypnotic Language Pattern Important To Learn

The basics of this pattern are very simple. The sentence is formed as "The more you X, the more you Y". In which, X is the action the listener will do no matter what, and Y is the action the speaker intends to influence the listener to do. The reason this structure is important is that it beautifully conveys the cause and effect relationship between X and Y without giving any hints of it. Persuasion psychologists have long pointed out that people tend to dislike being told to do something. When under the pressure to do other people's order, people have the tendency to resist it or deliberately do it in a wrong way. The "The more... the more" language structure efficiently makes the sentence appear like just a mere suggestions that the speaker wants the listeners to try out and see how it goes.

This hypnotic language pattern is important in that it's easily able to be used in most all life applications (e.g., "In an job position, the more I work in this company, the more you can be assured of my expertise; to the point of giving me a much higher rank in the organization. The more you use the product the more you realize its value and effectiveness —and, will keep coming back for more and more, time and time again.

It always helps you to persuade others, as it gives much more of a persuasive aspect to your tonality; making, you a much more confident and capable persuasive influencer.

What You Need To Know About This Hypnotic Language Pattern

Just like any other hypnotic language patterns, understanding when to use it and how to effectively apply it in different situations is very important. As mentioned earlier, speakers use this to subtly command the listeners to take an action in order to achieve a certain result. Since the structure is simple enough, learning to apply it naturally in a sentence or a part of the speech is not difficult. However, the more you practice doing it, the more you can use it intuitively.

Keep in mind: It is easily learnt and understood. It is also very relevant in almost all events and social environments. It can be used in almost all individual's life applications. It always comes out just so naturally, without much effort—making it easy for you to use as you need to.

How To Use This Hypnotic Language Pattern To Effectively Win People Over To Your Persuasions

Using this hypnotic language pattern in combination with other patterns can greatly increase your odds of winning people over to your persuasions. Firstly, when you use it to make constructive suggestions for the listeners regarding some good actions they can take to achieve good results, this structure emphasizes the positive notes in your suggestions, making it appear even brighter and more attractive to the listeners. Secondly, as explained earlier, people will not feel they are forced to do something against their wills. What they do is their own choice, and the more they do it, the more benefits they will receive.

"The more...The more" pattern can be used to achieve persuasion by indicating and giving the individual subject the rational thought that more advantages are achieved by continuing to do something more. This gives the addressed person eagerness and motivation to do more of the act in question that you want them to do; thus, persuading them to do more of it. Example: The more you continue doing your exercises the more weight you loose with time, to the point of achieving your dream size altogether.

How Else This Hypnotic Language Pattern Might Be Utilized Applicably In Other Useful Contexts

This pattern can be used in a wide variety of contexts, from persuading a customers to buy your goods/services, telling your children to do something, to convincing your potential employers to hire you. The only thing you need to bear in mind is to tailor it in each case and blend it successfully in your sentences. The more you examine different usages of the structure, the more you will get out of it.

Final Purport

In sum, 'The more____ the more____' is a very useful hypnotic language pattern that you can use to persuade someone to take some specific actions towards an intended result. To make it even more influential, you should learn to use it in combination with some other techniques. The more you combine it, for example, with the forthcoming hypnotic language patterns I'll be presenting you with in this book, the more likely you'll start using it to change minds and peoples' persuasions throughout the rest of your life—in a variety of contexts.

In this chapter, I shared with you an astonishingly hypnotic language pattern that you can use in a variety of contexts to produce far greater results persuasively. I explained that it would help you in persuasion, by making certain associations that were interconnected; yet, which did not have to be exactly 'tied' to each other to be perceived as associated. I then shared with you 'why' you should commit to learning and using this hypnotic language pattern; emphasizing on it effectiveness in the art of persuading individuals. Then I shared 'what' you needed to know about the hypnotic language pattern; namely: how to use it, how to formulate it, and where to apply it .After explaining what you needed to know, I explained step-by-step 'how' you can use this hypnotic language pattern to achieve the results you desire. Explicitly, I told you that step one meant doing the analysis of the set-up, that step two you should formulate the pattern, and step three you needed to deliver it. Lastly, we explored some other ways this hypnotic language pattern might be useful. We took an interdisciplinary approach and decided that this hypnotic language pattern could be used in other contexts such as sales, building one's career, and even in business applications where the goal is to produce results. Used in these contexts the benefits one might realize could include: many more sales, an increase in customer confidence, and overall 'better' terms of operation.

Action Steps

There is a principle someone taught me once, which they labeled the 'Law of Action'. It basically claims, that you can learn anything, be the most brilliant mind, but if you don't take what you know and put it into action, it's worthless. I'm guilty of this, so let me be first to raise my own hand.

For years I learned information from reading books, attending seminars, being a student (I have multiple degrees), and still I remained broke, and sometimes penniless.

Then I read a book, and got inspired to take action, and start sharing all this knowledge with others. I took a job as a sales trainer, and taught others what I knew, and not surprisingly the company I contracted to prospered abundantly. Then I started my own company, and began experiencing huge results. Today, I have a new habit: I take what I learn and teach it to others, for profit of course, and I love it. Action is my best friend, and was the missing ingredient in my life. Since I learned this law, I have never looked back, and my life has become a lot more meaningful, and more richly rewarded.

All of this being said, I encourage you to do the following action steps; not because I want to waste your time, but because I want you to have the results you want. You should maximize the value of this book, and earn an exponential return on your investment, my opinion anyway!

I.   Take this pattern and use it on ten people, and observe critically the response you're given by the other person. Watch for their physiology, their voice tonality, and what they actually say. More important usually is not what is said, but 'how' it's said. The word 'how' relates to energy or quality. When someone's response is congruently aligned with their physiology they are usually telling the truth, and resistance is lessened or non-existent. If someone tells you what you want to hear, but their physiology isn't congruently aligned, assume the opposite.

II.   Write a journal entry on your experiences using this 'exact' hypnotic language pattern. Note whether or not you got closer to your desired outcome, or further away. Also note if the person complied and took action or not.

III.   Make it a point to memorize this hypnotic language pattern now. The easiest way to do this is to use it on as many people as you can. Make it a part of your everyday language. Sooner or later you'll be using it unconsciously, and when you do you'll know that you're exactly where you need to be.

IV.   Teach this hypnotic language pattern to a friend or family member and explain what you've learned in this chapter to them. Perhaps

this person will be someone whom you can feed patterns back and forth off of, to help you master these 25 hypnotic language patterns sooner.

V. Get a 3x5 index card, and cut it in half vertically; namely, making two 'almost square' rectangles, and write this hypnotic language pattern on the front side. Below the pattern, make an abridged note to help you remember what contexts you should use the pattern in.

CHAPTER 4

Hypnotic Language Pattern Two of Twenty-Five

HYPNOTIC LANGUAGE PATTERN

____, AREN'T YOU?

Communication and interpersonal skills have become the two most sought-after qualities in this modern world. The answer to the question about how to improve your abilities to connect and persuade other people lies in the usage of hypnotic language patterns. One of the most common hypnotic language patterns used by many skillful speakers are tag questions. Tag questions are used very frequently by almost everyone, and those who master the use of tag questions also master a powerful hypnotic tool.

Why Is This Hypnotic Language Pattern Important To Learn

When talking to another person, or a group of people, the most important things are to engage them in the conversation, and then to win their approval. Tag questions enable you to achieve both goals. Many effective public speakers utilize this techniques when delivering their speech. People tend to lose attention and interest quickly if they do not feel like they are part of the conversation, and losing listeners' attention also means the speaker's failure. Therefore, by throwing in a tag question every now and then, waiting for a response from the audience, the speaker has a chance to gain back the attention. Why tag questions work more efficiently than other types of questions? It is because the speaker does not need a real answer, he only needs his audience to focus on his words and respond to what he has to say.

What You Need To Know About This Hypnotic Language Pattern

Putting a tag question at the end of a sentence is a lesson most people learn during their early school years. Hence, how to form a tag question should not be a big trouble for people. What you need to concentrate on is how to use it successfully as a hypnotic language pattern. Tag questions are most effective when used in combination with the right tone, facial expression, and in the right situation. Persuasive speakers know just the crucial moments to place a tag question, and stop for the response from their listener.

How To Use This Hypnotic Language Pattern To Effectively Win People Over To Your Persuasions

Generally, tag questions allow the speaker to form a deeper bond with the listener. The more nods and simple "yes/no" answers speakers receive, the more you can be certain that your audience will follow your words, share your experiences and understand what you are trying to convey. In addition, when skillfully placed at the end of a command statement, using the right tone and word choices, tag questions can also influence listeners' decisions, and make them lean towards what the speakers want them to believe. The speakers can hypnotically make listeners to say "yes" or agree to do what the speaker wants them to do before they even realize it.

How Else This Hypnotic Language Pattern Might Be Utilized Applicably In Other Useful Contexts

There are many contexts in which this hypnotic language pattern can be used to help the speaker influence their listeners. One great way to use is in small talks with almost anyone including your co-workers, family members, or clients. You also should explore to use it together with other language techniques to achieve an even greater impact. One thing to keep in mind is tag questions should not be overused because you do not want to appear aggressive or manipulative.

Final Purport

To sum it up, a tag question is a simple and useful trick to use when you want to form a relationship with your audience, based on agreement, and to influence the way they think. Practice makes it perfect so keep practicing it until you can use it in the most effective way, okay?

Action Steps

There is a principle someone taught me once, which they labeled the 'Law of Action'. It basically claims, that you can learn anything, be the most brilliant mind, but if you don't take what you know and put it into action, it's worthless. I'm guilty of this, so let me be first to raise my own hand.

For years I learned information from reading books, attending seminars, being a student (I have multiple degrees), and still I remained broke, and sometimes penniless.

Then I read a book, and got inspired to take action, and start sharing all this knowledge with others. I took a job as a sales trainer, and taught others what I knew, and not surprisingly the company I contracted to prospered abundantly. Then I started my own company, and began experiencing huge results. Today, I have a new habit: I take what I learn and teach it to others, for profit of course, and I love it. Action is my best friend, and was the missing ingredient in my life. Since I learned this law, I have never looked back, and my life has become a lot more meaningful, and more richly rewarded.

All of this being said, I encourage you to do the following action steps; not because I want to waste your time, but because I want you to have the results you want. You should maximize the value of this book, and earn an exponential return on your investment, my opinion anyway!

I. Take this pattern and use it on ten people, and observe critically the response you're given by the other person. Watch for their physiology, their voice tonality, and what they actually say. More important usually is not what is said, but 'how' it's said. The word 'how' relates to energy or quality. When someone's response is congruently aligned with their physiology they are usually telling the truth, and resistance is lessened or non-existent. If someone tells you what you want to hear, but their physiology isn't congruently aligned, assume the opposite.

II. Write a journal entry on your experiences using this 'exact' hypnotic language pattern. Note whether or not you got closer to your desired

outcome, or further away. Also note if the person complied and took action or not.

III.   Make it a point to memorize this hypnotic language pattern now. The easiest way to do this is to use it on as many people as you can. Make it a part of your everyday language. Sooner or later you'll be using it unconsciously, and when you do you'll know that you're exactly where you need to be.

IV.   Teach this hypnotic language pattern to a friend or family member and explain what you've learned in this chapter to them. Perhaps this person will be someone whom you can feed patterns back and forth off of, to help you master these 25 hypnotic language patterns sooner.

V.   Get a 3x5 index card, and cut it in half vertically; namely, making two 'almost square' rectangles, and write this hypnotic language pattern on the front side. Below the pattern, make an abridged note to help you remember what contexts you should use the pattern in.

Hypnotic Language Pattern Three of Twenty-Five

HYPNOTIC LANGUAGE PATTERN

<u>*MANY*</u> *PEOPLE* ___.

Why some people can deliver a speech more persuasively than others? As more researches have been conducted on hypnotic language patterns, people have also become more aware of their existence and the impact those patterns can have on the art of persuasion when integrating skillfully into one's sentences. Among them, universal quantifiers have been received special attention as being one of the most convenient and simplest hypnotic language patterns. Besides being used frequently in almost all conversations, universal quantifiers also enable speakers to influence their listeners in a very unique and powerful way.

Why Is This Hypnotic Language Pattern Important To Learn

Almost everyone knows what quantifiers are. Quantifiers refer to such words as *many, some, few, none, most of,* and so on. Universal quantifiers always carry in itself a note of exaggeration, and vagueness. What makes this hypnotic language pattern important is that it efficiently implies the idea of generalization without revealing any trace of it. Much psychological research has concluded that people have the tendency to want to be a part of a group or tribe, and tend to think the same way other people think. It is up to debate whether this is a good characteristic, but many masterful speakers aim to take advantage of this group-think tendency to influence their audience. For example, the speaker might say most of his or her successful customers use the product he or she offers. In this case, the listener will be more likely to agree so that he or she will be accepted in the group of 'successful customers'.

What You Need To Know About This Hypnotic Language Pattern

In order to make the most of this hypnotic language pattern, you need to learn how to choose the correct quantifiers wisely and pay attention to the noun phrases and verbs that go directly after the quantifiers. Positive expressions are used to encourage listeners to take the actions the speakers intend to influence the listeners to take, and vice versa, negative expressions are used to discourage listeners from doing something. In both cases, knowing just the right place and moment to insert the statement into the conversation is also the key to success.

How To Use This Hypnotic Language Pattern To Effectively Win People Over To Your Persuasions

As mentioned earlier, quantifiers help speakers to win other people's approval by arousing their desire to be part of a group. Also, due to the vague nature of the language, it exaggerates the credibility of what the speaker says. For example, when the speaker say almost all of his clients recommended his products to their friends and family, the listener only assumes that "almost all" means a lot of people, almost everyone, and then to the speaker's advantage, the listener might further assume that he will, like everyone else, enjoy the product and recommend it to others. The listener never questions "almost all" includes how many people exactly.

How Else This Hypnotic Language Pattern Might Be Utilized Applicably In Other Useful Contexts

Quantifiers can be used in so many contexts to help you influence others people as long as you know how to use it effectively. Salespeople can use it in their sales pitch with clients, and employers can use it to convince their employees to do or not do something. What's more, you can even use it to motivate yourself and other people to do something. Mottoes such as "Every person I know can do it, I can do it as well" can work very well in reinforcing your determination to complete a task.

Final Purport

Although it is a very simple hypnotic language pattern, universal quantifier can go great lengths in convincing people. In order to make it more influential, you can practice combining quantifiers with other patterns, and applying them to a wide variety of contexts to see when they work best.

Action Steps

There is a principle someone taught me once, which they labeled the 'Law of Action'. It basically claims, that you can learn anything, be the most brilliant mind, but if you don't take what you know and put it into action, it's worthless. I'm guilty of this, so let me be first to raise my own hand.

For years I learned information from reading books, attending seminars, being a student (I have multiple degrees), and still I remained broke, and sometimes penniless.

Then I read a book, and got inspired to take action, and start sharing all this knowledge with others. I took a job as a sales trainer, and taught others what I knew, and not surprisingly the company I contracted to prospered abundantly. Then I started my own company, and began experiencing huge results. Today, I have a new habit: I take what I learn and teach it to others, for profit of course, and I love it. Action is my best friend, and was the missing ingredient in my life. Since I learned this law, I have never looked back, and my life has become a lot more meaningful, and more richly rewarded.

All of this being said, I encourage you to do the following action steps; not because I want to waste your time, but because I want you to have the results you want. You should maximize the value of this book, and earn an exponential return on your investment, my opinion anyway!

I. Take this pattern and use it on ten people, and observe critically the response you're given by the other person. Watch for their physiology, their voice tonality, and what they actually say. More important usually is not what is said, but 'how' it's said. The word 'how' relates to energy or quality. When someone's response is congruently aligned with their physiology they are usually telling the truth, and resistance is lessened or non-existent. If someone tells you what you want to hear, but their physiology isn't congruently aligned, assume the opposite.

II.   Write a journal entry on your experiences using this 'exact' hypnotic language pattern. Note whether or not you got closer to your desired outcome, or further away. Also note if the person complied and took action or not.

III.   Make it a point to memorize this hypnotic language pattern now. The easiest way to do this is to use it on as many people as you can. Make it a part of your everyday language. Sooner or later you'll be using it unconsciously, and when you do you'll know that you're exactly where you need to be.

IV.   Teach this hypnotic language pattern to a friend or family member and explain what you've learned in this chapter to them. Perhaps this person will be someone whom you can feed patterns back and forth off of, to help you master these 25 hypnotic language patterns sooner.

Get a 3x5 index card, and cut it in half vertically; namely, making two 'almost square' rectangles, and write this hypnotic language pattern on the front side. Below the pattern, make an abridged note to help you remember what contexts you should use the pattern in.

CHAPTER 6

Hypnotic Language Pattern Four of Twenty-Five

HYPNOTIC LANGUAGE PATTERN

EMBEDDED COMMAND PATTERN

Have you ever wonder why some people can easily ask you to do something for them without ever appearing bossy or dominating? One reason can be because those people are experts in using embedded command, one of the most popular hypnotic language patterns. Instead of making a short and obvious command, the speaker deftly hide his command in a larger sentence without making the listener language pattern is a very powerful one, and can be applied to various useful contexts.

Why Is This Hypnotic Language Pattern Important To Learn

This pattern is very important to know, and in fact, almost all successful hypnotists and effective speakers master the use of it and apply it on a regular basis. One reason that makes it a powerful pattern is that it manipulates the conscious part of the human mind and enables the embedded command to go straight into the unconscious part of the mind.

When being ordered to do something, the conscious mind quickly grasps the order, analyzes it, and has the initial reaction as to deny or resist it. People tend to dislike being told what to do, and that tendency is even more pronounced today when kids are educated since their early childhood to think critically and independently. The embedded command finds a way to bypass the stubborn conscious mind by using a larger sentence, leading the listener to focus on the bigger picture and naturally accepting the command.

What You Need To Know About This Hypnotic Language Pattern

Unlike some other hypnotic language patterns such as universal quantifiers and tag questions, embedded commands require more practice to be able to completely master it. The foundation of embedded commands is to come up with a command, preferably with less than five words, and embed it into a larger sentence which naturally and persuasively fit into a conversation. For example, instead of ordering someone with "Do X", you will say something like "You may wonder if do X will do you any good, I can tell you that many people do X and find it very beneficial". Another thing you need to know about this pattern is that you should never use any words or phrases associated with that of the actual command, which might trigger the conscious mind to realize the hidden command.

If you happen to do this, chances are you'll lose all rapport you've built with your subject, and they will suspect you of 'trying' to influence them. Remember, these hypnotic language patterns are 'indirect' and 'covert' and go under the radar of your subject's conscious mind. You have to be very natural in your delivery, because if you get caught using these patterns, to someone who might put 2 and 2 together, then you'll lose the sale, put the relationship with that person into a state of disrepair, and possibly worst. Being artfully vague is the best way to be. It is better that your subject think you're a bit 'slow' than to think you're a 'persuasion artist'—out to control and manipulate them. Just be careful is all I'm saying. This particular hypnotic language pattern takes time to master well, so don't rush the process. Taking your time, and developing good habits early on, will take your farther, quicker. My point: Sometimes you have to go slow, to go fast.

How To Use This Hypnotic Language Pattern To Effectively Win People Over To Your Persuasions

The final purpose of this pattern is to persuade people to do what the speaker wants them to do by making their mind imagine and concentrate on other parts of the sentence, not the command itself. The brighter and more convincing picture the speaker can paint, the more likely that the listener will agree to do what the speaker commands him or her to do. Embedded commands will have an even greater impact when combined with other strategies such as using the right tone and nodding. When used correctly, speakers can easily achieve their goal of influencing others to accept their persuasions.

Also, keep in mind that you want to 'analogue mark' your embedded commands: Meaning you want to pause before and after the command is delivered. Take for example the embedded command: 'read this book'. You want to first of all nest it into your conversation, typically by placing it inside a larger sentence or compound sentence. For example: When you 'read this book', you'll discover how easy it is to hypnotize anyone by simply having a seemingly ordinary conversation, wouldn't you say? Notice how I have analogue marked the embedded command with single quotation marks, i.e. 'read this book'. These single quotation marks represent the pauses I would be making subtly just before stating the hidden indirect command.

Even though the subject doesn't consciously pick up on this subtleness, their hypnotic mind or 'subconscious' does, and it follows it out precisely; even though the subject is completely unaware that they are following your command. To them—they simply think it is their idea to do the action.

How Else This Hypnotic Language Pattern Might Be Utilized Applicably In Other Useful Contexts

Hypnotists, psychologists, and mental health counselor use very often use the embedded command hypnotic language pattern in their treatment to persuade their patients to take a specific actions. Besides professional use, in your daily life, there are many situations when you need to ask someone to do something for you; whether it is to ask your children to do homework, your spouse to help you with housework, your co-worker to cooperate and assist you with some tasks, or your clients to buy your products/ services. In those cases, embedded command is one of the hypnotic language patterns that will enable you to effectively persuade people to take actions.

Final Purport

As mentioned earlier, embedded command is a very useful hypnotic language pattern, but it is quite a hard one to learn and apply. Therefore, if you want to use it, spend some time doing some more research on the best practices and try to apply it whenever the opportunity arises. Practice will help you immensely when it comes to delivering the embedded command in just the perfect way. I personally think the best part about using this hypnotic language pattern is in how eager people are to want to comply with the command you've covertly injected into their hypnotic mind (subconscious). When they believe, without even thinking about it that it is their idea they're acting on, it is interesting to watch them claim ownership of the idea, which is actually a command you gave them.

Action Steps

There is a principle someone taught me once, which they labeled the 'Law of Action'. It basically claims, that you can learn anything, be the most brilliant mind, but if you don't take what you know and put it into action, it's worthless. I'm guilty of this, so let me be first to raise my own hand.

For years I learned information from reading books, attending seminars, being a student (I have multiple degrees), and still I remained broke, and sometimes penniless.

Then I read a book, and got inspired to take action, and start sharing all this knowledge with others. I took a job as a sales trainer, and taught others what I knew, and not surprisingly the company I contracted to prospered abundantly. Then I started my own company, and began experiencing huge results. Today, I have a new habit: I take what I learn and teach it to others, for profit of course, and

I love it. Action is my best friend, and was the missing ingredient in my life. Since I learned this law, I have never looked back, and my life has become a lot more meaningful, and more richly rewarded.

All of this being said, I encourage you to do the following action steps; not because I want to waste your time, but because I want you to have the results you want. You should maximize the value of this book, and earn an exponential return on your investment, my opinion anyway!

I.   Take this pattern and use it on ten people, and observe critically the response you're given by the other person. Watch for their physiology, their voice tonality, and what they actually say. More important usually is not what is said, but 'how' it's said. The word 'how' relates to energy or quality. When someone's response is congruently aligned with their physiology they are usually telling the truth, and resistance is lessened or non-existent. If someone tells you what you want to hear, but their physiology isn't congruently aligned, assume the opposite.

II.   Write a journal entry on your experiences using this 'exact' hypnotic language pattern. Note whether or not you got closer to your desired outcome, or further away. Also note if the person complied and took action or not.

III. Make it a point to memorize this hypnotic language pattern now. The easiest way to do this is to use it on as many people as you can. Make it a part of your everyday language. Sooner or later you'll be using it unconsciously, and when you do you'll know that you're exactly where you need to be.

IV. Teach this hypnotic language pattern to a friend or family member and explain what you've learned in this chapter to them. Perhaps this person will be someone whom you can feed patterns back and forth off of, to help you master these 25 hypnotic language patterns sooner.

V. Get a 3x5 index card, and cut it in half vertically; namely, making two 'almost square' rectangles, and write this hypnotic language pattern on the front side. Below the pattern, make an abridged note to help you remember what contexts you should use the pattern in.

CHAPTER 7

Hypnotic Language Pattern Five of Twenty-Five

HYPNOTIC LANGUAGE PATTERN

THAT'S INTERESTING...

...TELL ME MORE

...WHY WOULD YOU SAY THAT

...WHY WOULD YOU DO THAT

...WHY WOULD YOU ASK THAT

It is not uncommon that you'll be inundated with a question from time to time. They have a saying in sales: Whoever is asking the questions is in control. This point can't be underscored enough. The problem, however, is if you answer a question with a question many people will instantly assume you're trying to 'dodge' the question. As a result, they'll start to clam up, and close down on you. For this reason, you want to be able to artfully answer a question with a question, but leading with the hypnotic language pattern: That's interesting. After you lead with a statement, you're then allowed by the rules of social etiquette to ask another question back to them.

Why Is This Hypnotic Language Pattern Important To Learn

To be candid, learning this hypnotic language pattern will make it so you never have to worry about finding yourself in a position where you don't know what to say, when asked a question. Not all questions are easy question to reply back to. For example, if you ever find yourself being interrogated by someone, they line of questioning they're using may not only intimidate you, but also cause you to lose control of the conversation and say more than you should. People could judge you, lose faith in you, not want to do business with you, or believe somewhere in their minds that you're less than honest, or trying to pull the wool over their eyes or something like this.

To ensure you never offend someone, and always know what to say, and specifically how to respond to someone's difficult to hear questions, you'll want to use this hypnotic language pattern.

The pattern is hypnotic from the word 'interesting' as anything or anyone can be interesting or have some interesting characteristic. Interesting comes from the infinitive verb 'to have interest'. The nominalized verb gets conjugated into the noun 'interest'. This is a safe word, i.e. interesting, because it is not uncommon for somebody to be interested in something and then suddenly lose interest. And, for this reason, using the word interesting to lead with, tells the other person you're not only paying attention to them, yet that you value them and find what they have to say or ask as 'interesting'—nobody wants to be perceived as 'boring'. Boring is the antonym of interesting, by the way.

What You Need To Know About This Hypnotic Language Pattern

Specifically, you need to know that the lead is a statement; namely, "That's interesting". You are not really saying much when you say this. You are in a positive way, however, declaring that you find what was asked of you as being interesting. This is a positive way to start an answer, yet you need something more.

That something more is another question; yet, specifically, a 'follow-up' or 'clarification' question. These types of questions help you uncover more in detail what the questioner really intentioned for you to answer.

Now this is important, because when you ask a follow-up question, it forces the question-asker to ask what they asked you in a little bit different way. In other words, you force them to 'reframe' the question and present it in a different way.

The follow-up or clarification questions can be any one of four questions. Each will work for a different context or type of question you may be asked. This is a critical distinction to take note of, because knowing all four of these follow-up questions will ensure you never have to hesitate or wonder what question to ask. One of the four questions will work for any situation you might find yourself in.

These four follow-up questions are: (a) Tell me more, (b) Why would you say that, (c) Why would you do that, and (d) Why would you ask that? Each of them will get you out of any type of challenging interpersonal communication scenario you might find yourself in.

How To Use This Hypnotic Language Pattern To Effectively Win People Over To Your Persuasions

Perhaps the best way to learn how to apply this hypnotic language pattern is to imagine someone asking you a difficult question. Think about a question you don't want someone asking you. Think up a specific person, and keep them in your mind, as you contemplate a question you wouldn't want this person asking you. Once you have that person and question in mind, pretend that you are somewhere with them, and that they ask you this exact question.

Now that you have this situation in mind, answer with: "That's interesting." And then pause, and ask whichever follow-up question seems to work best for the context and situation.

I know someone recently who asked me a question I simply didn't feel like answering them back on. I couldn't exactly get out of answering, because this person is a close friend of the family, who meant well, even though they intended on cornering me in an argument that most people would lose by responding to. I used this exact same approach:

My friend asked, "Why didn't you come to your sister's work party? Were you trying to get out of helping her? She said you weren't busy, and seemed upset. Why didn't you come?"

I responded with: "That's interesting…" I paused and said, "Why would you ask me that?"

My friend, was shell-shocked and now on the defensive side of the fence. He finally responded with: "Yeah…You're right. None of my business. I'm sorry, I shouldn't have even brought this up."

The rest of our coffee break was smooth sailing and we went on talking about all sorts of cool things that brought some positivity back into the conversation. My point for sharing this story with you is to simply show you how to use the hypnotic language pattern, while also giving you a case study type example so you can understand the effect this pattern had on my particular situation.

How Else This Hypnotic Language Pattern Might Be Utilized Applicably In Other Useful Contexts

This pattern is a 'get out of jail card' in my opinion. It saves you from those tricky conversations where someone wants to be argumentative or to where someone wants to ask you some very serious questions you don't want to answer. By adopting this hypnotic language patter you're essentially achieving the result of having them cross the line into territory that is socially unacceptable. Once they cross that line, they are not getting any more information out of you. You're also not required to respond at that point with any type of detailed response.

For this reason you can use this hypnotic language pattern to ensure people don't ask you personal or uncomfortable questions in the future—because they will have realized it's not in their best interest to do so. In other words, this language pattern sets the stage for halting future incidences where the same person may try and engage you in a personal attack or ask you a question you really don't feel like answering, or that's not socially appropriate.

Final Purport

To recap, there are times in life when someone may attempt to ask you questions that you don't want to be asked. It may, for them, as far as the situation is concerned, be a socially acceptable question to ask, that's most often reasonable.

You still may not want to be asked the question—let alone answer it! The good news is you don't have to answer these types of questions, when you follow the simple formula we went over in this chapter.

All you really have to do is say, "That's interesting," then pause, and ask or reply: (a) "Why would you ask me that?" (b) "Why would you do that?" (c) "Why would you say that?" or (d) "Tell me more about that?"

These clarifying questions and 'tell me more' statement are helpful for getting to the underlying meaning of 'why' the person is asking you that question. Once you know 'why' you can easily spin the answer in a way that either puts them on the defensive or having more information give an answer you don't mind giving.

Action Steps

There is a principle someone taught me once, which they labeled the 'Law of Action'. It basically claims, that you can learn anything, be the most brilliant mind, but if you don't take what you know and put it into action, it's worthless. I'm guilty of this, so let me be first to raise my own hand.

For years I learned information from reading books, attending seminars, being a student (I have multiple degrees), and still I remained broke, and sometimes penniless.

Then I read a book, and got inspired to take action, and start sharing all this knowledge with others. I took a job as a sales trainer, and taught others what I knew, and not surprisingly the company I contracted to prospered abundantly. Then I started my own company, and began experiencing huge results. Today, I have a new habit: I take what I learn and teach it to others, for profit of course, and I love it. Action is my best friend, and was the missing ingredient in my life. Since I learned this law, I have never looked back, and my life has become a lot more meaningful, and more richly rewarded.

All of this being said, I encourage you to do the following action steps; not because I want to waste your time, but because I want you to have the results you want. You should maximize the value of this book, and earn an exponential return on your investment, my opinion anyway!

I. Take this pattern and use it on ten people, and observe critically the response you're given by the other person. Watch for their physiology, their voice tonality, and what they actually say. More important usually is not what is said, but 'how' it's said. The word 'how' relates to energy or quality. When someone's response is congruently aligned with their physiology they are usually telling the truth, and resistance is lessened or non-existent. If someone tells you what you want to hear, but their physiology isn't congruently aligned, assume the opposite.

II. Write a journal entry on your experiences using this 'exact' hypnotic language pattern. Note whether or not you got closer to your desired outcome, or further away. Also note if the person complied and took action or not.

III. Make it a point to memorize this hypnotic language pattern now. The easiest way to do this is to use it on as many people as you can. Make it a part of your everyday language. Sooner or later you'll be using it unconsciously, and when you do you'll know that you're exactly where you need to be.

IV. Teach this hypnotic language pattern to a friend or family member and explain what you've learned in this chapter to them. Perhaps this person will be someone whom you can feed patterns back and forth off of, to help you master these 25 hypnotic language patterns sooner.

V. Get a 3x5 index card, and cut it in half vertically; namely, making two 'almost square' rectangles, and write this hypnotic language pattern on the front side. Below the pattern, make an abridged note to help you remember what contexts you should use the pattern in.

CHAPTER 8

Hypnotic Language Pattern Six of Twenty-Five

HYPNOTIC LANGUAGE PATTERN

THE NON-VERBAL HYPNOTIC LANGUAGE PATTERN

Over the years hypnotic language patterns have elicited a lot of interest with the various types being embraced by people interested in communications or passing information across.

In this chapter, I will critically outline how the non-verbal hypnotic language pattern 'body language' can be used to break various communication barriers for individuals to understand one another without saying a word to one another. Basically human beings are skeptical in nature and they usually weigh their options before they act;

making them more rational than other animals. Being skeptical prior to taking action displays a wait and see attitude which means there are several options with different consequences that one has to consider before making a move. Making the right decision, according to this hypnotic language pattern is a way of achieving the end results with ease which many people strive for in building relationships.

The importance of the hypnotic language pattern is that in real life, people are confronted with many options to choose from especially what they like about others especially in the dating realm. Making the right decision on the right partner is equally important. There is always the fear of failure or being rejected hence the thought of what if they don't like me, we might hurt each other, maybe something may go wrong or what if I take a different approach, will the plan work?

Many successful entrepreneurs on the other hand take this non-verbal hypnotic language pattern and can read both conscious and sub-consciously active when discussing business with their prospects. Through the non-verbal body language, one is able to tell whether a deal is a deal or a no deal. It is a tool used by sales people in the field when introducing and selling their products and services. Others opt for some research before taking the risks involved—for fear of failure.

A simple smile—for example—can make a big difference. It can break huge communication barriers making it easier to exchange ideas and information, which in turn makes strangers or foes become acquaintances. Body language is undoubtedly one of the best ways of expressing acceptance or rejection. Learning its basics is a surefire way of understanding other people either in business, relationships or across cultural diversity.

Why Is This Hypnotic Language Pattern Important To Learn

There are many reasons why nonverbal body language is important. It is critical to understand each and every body movement since each different messages. A wink for instance might imply acceptance or doubt thus the need for clear understanding and prevailing mood or circumstances.

Learning body language as a hypnotic pattern help people understand each other's feelings, wants, aspirations and, needs as well. People are socialized differently and learning this form of language eliminates culture shock.

What You Need To Know About This Hypnotic Language Pattern

This is one of the most contagious language and does not have any boundaries. It does not discriminate between the young and old nor the mighty and the lowly. It helps in building trust not only to people you are close to but strangers as well. It is founded on the premise that a stranger is the one whose body language you do not understand at the very moment you meet them.

You also need to know that a person's body language happens to occur at the unconscious level. Observe your body language right now, at this very moment, and I'm sure you'll find yourself making a movement without any justifiable reason or logic for making that movement. One thing for sure is that you're always creating body movements that are unconscious, as well as conscious. Your breathing, your heart pumping, your finger movements, the crossing of your legs, or not, all are unconscious body movements that happen under the radar of consciousness.

Our body language gives us away! Our non-verbal communication communicates more than our verbal language patterns. After you master people's body language and what it means, you'll actually know someone better than they know themselves. What's more, you'll be able to predict their behavior, just by the way they communicate to you unconsciously through their non-verbal hypnotic language.

How To Use This Hypnotic Language Pattern To Effectively Win People Over To Your Persuasions

Since this a nonverbal language, you can choose actions that are easily understood to win others. Some of the most persuasive acts include and not limited to thumbs up, smile, winks, pat on the back, as well as, when appropriate—hugs. Choosing the right body language at the right moment is very important as it sends the right message at the right time thus winning others over in a polite and dignified manner. This can be in meetings, the workplace or even during social gatherings.

You'll also want to test when a particular nonverbal hypnotic language pattern is appropriate or not, so you can determine predictively what is appropriate and likely to happen as a result, and what isn't likely. Different context will require different nonverbal cues.

How Else This Hypnotic Language Pattern Might Be Utilized Applicably In Other Useful Contexts

There are many ways one can take effective advantage of using body language. Eye contact in dating has always been used to externalize ones feelings and trebling lips is a sure way of yearning for a genuine kiss. Additionally, body language pattern has been used in interview sessions to ascertain a candidate's credibility. Many interviewees portray the wrong body language and end up falling despite being articulate in other aspects.

Courtrooms are other places where body language patterns play a major role in determining whether one is guilty or otherwise. Judges may look at the body posture and partly base their final judgment on it. Last but not least, psychologically, body language patterns have been used to intimidate opponents in games and some lose out of misunderstood body signs thus winners taking advantage of body language understanding.

Final Purport

Body language is another hypnotic language pattern used as a tool to influence others to conform to your intentions. When used appropriately as a communication tool, it creates trust among people of different opinions thus harmonizing their thoughts and feelings as well. With clear understanding, this form of hypnotic language pattern is beneficial in relationship building; yet, when misunderstood or misused—it can break relationships before they take form. Some institutions and individuals use this language pattern to their benefit. It has proved to be a powerful tool in bringing out the truth in people.

Action Steps

There is a principle someone taught me once, which they labeled the 'Law of Action'. It basically claims, that you can learn anything, be the most brilliant mind, but if you don't take what you know and put it into action, it's worthless. I'm guilty of this, so let me be first to raise my own hand.

For years I learned information from reading books, attending seminars, being a student (I have multiple degrees), and still I remained broke, and sometimes penniless.

Then I read a book, and got inspired to take action, and start sharing all this knowledge with others. I took a job as a sales trainer, and taught others what I knew, and not

surprisingly the company I contracted to prospered abundantly. Then I started my own company, and began experiencing huge results. Today, I have a new habit: I take what I learn and teach it to others, for profit of course, and I love it. Action is my best friend, and was the missing ingredient in my life. Since I learned this law, I have never looked back, and my life has become a lot more meaningful, and more richly rewarded.

All of this being said, I encourage you to do the following action steps; not because I want to waste your time, but because I want you to have the results you want. You should maximize the value of this book, and earn an exponential return on your investment, my opinion anyway!

I.   Take this pattern and use it on ten people, and observe critically the response you're given by the other person. Watch for their physiology, their voice tonality, and what they actually say. More important usually is not what is said, but 'how' it's said. The word 'how' relates to energy or quality. When someone's response is congruently aligned with their physiology they are usually telling the truth, and resistance is lessened or non-existent. If someone tells you what you want to hear, but their physiology isn't congruently aligned, assume the opposite.

II.   Write a journal entry on your experiences using this 'exact' hypnotic language pattern. Note whether or not you got closer to your desired

outcome, or further away. Also note if the person complied and took action or not.

III.   Make it a point to memorize this hypnotic language pattern now. The easiest way to do this is to use it on as many people as you can. Make it a part of your everyday language. Sooner or later you'll be using it unconsciously, and when you do you'll know that you're exactly where you need to be.

IV.   Teach this hypnotic language pattern to a friend or family member and explain what you've learned in this chapter to them. Perhaps this person will be someone whom you can feed patterns back and forth off of, to help you master these 25 hypnotic language patterns sooner.

V.   Get a 3x5 index card, and cut it in half vertically; namely, making two 'almost square' rectangles, and write this hypnotic language pattern on the front side. Below the pattern, make an abridged note to help you remember what contexts you should use the pattern in.

Hypnotic Language Pattern Seven of Twenty-Five

HYPNOTIC LANGUAGE PATTERN

THE ISSUE ISN'T ___, IT'S ___.

Sometimes people find themselves in a conversation in which both sides just keep arguing endlessly over a matter that none of them is willing to compromise. One thing a clever speaker can do is to shift the attention skillfully from the useless controversial topic to another matter that looks more promising and both sides can easily agree upon. A hypnotic language pattern that can enable you to do that is the pattern "The issue isn't... It's..." This is a powerful pattern and can be used in various contexts to help the user win over a debate.

Why Is This Hypnotic Language Pattern Important To Learn

The basic of the structure is very simple, but it will take some practice to completely master it. The sentence is formed as "The issue isn't X, it's Y". In which X is the argument that the other person use to argue with you and Y is the matter that you attempt to make him or her concentrate on. This hypnotic language pattern is so important because it makes the listener lose their guard, and switch their attention the other matter that the speaker just brings up or Y. It helps the speaker to avoid unnecessary and never-ending bickering, delete the original argument from the listener's mind, and replace them with another one that the speaker can handle more easily. The pattern also takes advantage of the fact pointed out by some psychological research that human's working memory is short-term, and people tend to remember and focus more on the last part of the things they hear.

What You Need To Know About This Hypnotic Language Pattern

The formula for this pattern is quite straightforward. There are two things the speakers need to know in order to master the use of it. First, the speaker needs to know exactly when to use this strategy and this also needs some skills and experiences. When the speaker decides from the conversation that there is no way he can satisfactorily and persuasively answer the other person's argument directly, it will be the right time to use this phrase. Second, he also needs to come up with another convincing argument to paint a brighter picture for his or her listener to look at. With the right reason, a persuasive tone, and a confident attitude, the speaker can convince the listener to agree with his new argument.

How To Use This Hypnotic Language Pattern To Effectively Win People Over To Your Persuasions

One way your can use this hypnotic language pattern is to turn the listener's focus from his concern to your reason, which works to your advantages. For example if your customer complains about your hotel's inconvenient location, you can make the argument that "The issue isn't about our faraway location. It's about your being able to be closer to the nature, and enjoy the fresh air of the mountains." This deletes the memory of an inconvenient location from the customer's mind and makes them to concentrate only the beautiful picture of fresh air and beautiful nature. Another way you can use it is to shift listener's attention to a different time frame. For example, if your client argues that your products are too expensive, you can persuading them by saying "The issue isn't about how much it costs you now, it's about how much you can save in the next two weeks". By making the future looks promising, the speaker can make the listener more willing to accept the problem in the present.

How Else This Hypnotic Language Pattern Might Be Utilized Applicably In Other Useful Contexts

This pattern can be applied in many other contexts to help you win over the debate without having to fight directly with other people. Salespeople can utilize it to convince their customers to tolerate the cost of the products at present to enjoy more benefits in the future. Another useful context to apply this structure is in customer services to counter the customers' complaint about a certain feature of a product by pointing them towards other strong features and advantages of that product. The keys to success of this strategy are choosing the right argument, and appearing confident and professional.

Final Purport

Body language is another hypnotic language pattern used as a tool to influence others to conform to your intentions. When used appropriately as a communication tool, it creates trust among people of different opinions thus harmonizing their thoughts and feelings as well. With clear understanding, this form of hypnotic language pattern is beneficial in relationship building; yet, when misunderstood or misused—it can break relationships before they take form. Some institutions and individuals use this language pattern to their benefit. It has proved to be a powerful tool in bringing out the truth in people.

Action Steps

There is a principle someone taught me once, which they labeled the 'Law of Action'. It basically claims, that you can learn anything, be the most brilliant mind, but if you don't take what you know and put it into action, it's worthless. I'm guilty of this, so let me be first to raise my own hand.

For years I learned information from reading books, attending seminars, being a student (I have multiple degrees), and still I remained broke, and sometimes penniless.

Then I read a book, and got inspired to take action, and start sharing all this knowledge with others. I took a job as a sales trainer, and taught others what I knew, and not surprisingly the company I contracted to prospered abundantly. Then I started my own company, and began experiencing huge results. Today, I have a new habit: I take what I learn and teach it to others, for profit of course, and I love it. Action is my best friend, and was the missing ingredient in my life. Since I learned this law, I have never looked back, and my life has become a lot more meaningful, and more richly rewarded.

All of this being said, I encourage you to do the following action steps; not because I want to waste your time, but because I want you to have the results you want. You should maximize the value of this book, and earn an exponential return on your investment, my opinion anyway!

I.   Take this pattern and use it on ten people, and observe critically the response you're given by the other person. Watch for their physiology, their voice tonality, and what they actually say. More important usually is not what is said, but 'how' it's said. The word 'how' relates to energy or quality. When someone's response is congruently aligned with their physiology they are usually telling the truth, and resistance is lessened or non-existent. If someone tells you what you want to hear, but their physiology isn't congruently aligned, assume the opposite.

II.   Write a journal entry on your experiences using this 'exact' hypnotic language pattern. Note whether or not you got closer to your desired outcome, or further away. Also note if the person complied and took action or not.

III.   Make it a point to memorize this hypnotic language pattern now. The easiest way to do this is to use it on as many people as you can. Make it a part of your everyday language. Sooner or later you'll be using it unconsciously, and when you do you'll know that you're exactly where you need to be.

IV. Teach this hypnotic language pattern to a friend or family member and explain what you've learned in this chapter to them. Perhaps this person will be someone whom you can feed patterns back and forth off of, to help you master these 25 hypnotic language patterns sooner.

V. Get a 3x5 index card, and cut it in half vertically; namely, making two 'almost square' rectangles, and write this hypnotic language pattern on the front side. Below the pattern, make an abridged note to help you remember what contexts you should use the pattern in.

Hypnotic Language Pattern Eight of Twenty-Five

HYPNOTIC LANGUATE PATTERN

MODAL OPERATOR PATTERN

Hypnotic Language Patterns, also referred to as Milton Model Patterns, are based on an indirect form of hypnosis that utilizes the voice and words in order to persuade the mind and influence the subconscious. These patterns were developed after the discovery that renowned hypnotherapist Milton Erickson utilized various forms of speech and vocabulary in order to bypass his patients' conscious thoughts and critical nature. One of the patterns in the Milton Model is the Modal Operator Pattern. This chapter will explain the importance of this pattern and why it is relevant. It will also inform the reader about important facts and details regarding Modal Operators. Finally, the chapter will explore other instances and situations where this particular pattern might be useful and beneficial.

Why Is This Hypnotic Language Pattern Important To Learn

The Modal Operator Hypnotic Language Pattern is important to learn because it deals with individual rules and personal boundaries. The terms: can, should, would, have, need, can't, shouldn't, and wouldn't are extremely common to this particular pattern. Discovering what a person's limits are enables an individual to make suggestions or give advice in order to influence their thoughts. It also allows them to subtly introduce new ideas and possibilities as a way to push the limits and expand them by creating feelings of necessity.

What You Need To Know About This Hypnotic Language Pattern

Everyone in general has an internal set of core values or rules that they operate their lives around. Some are very strict while others are much more lenient. All are learned and developed through one's own life experiences and perceptions. More often than not, a person will make decisions based on their past occurrences and the resulting feelings that are formed around those experiences.

This hypnotic language pattern is useful for the conversational hypnotist, because these patterns, i.e. should, shouldn't, must, mustn't, have to, need, and so on are used linguistically in conversations to put stress and emphasis on beliefs (whether true or not) that a subject has. By 'subject' of course I mean anyone you're conversationally hypnotizing. I've used this term throughout this book, and others, to designate 'every' context and 'individual' in which you find yourself conversationally hypnotizing someone.

How To Use This Hypnotic Language Pattern To Effectively Win People Over To Your Persuasions

Changing a person's perception is no easy task. As the old saying goes "You never get a second chance to make a first impression". When someone has an idea or belief about something they will generally cling to it rather strongly. However, if they do not feel they are going against themselves or feel there is a better alternative or another way to view the situation, it leaves the door open for suggestion which can result in being persuaded to change the mind. Some are more easily swayed than others. It depends a lot on personality, confidence, mental capacity, and how strong the belief is.

Anytime you have two or more people in discussion, influence is happening. We influence others; as well as are influenced by others. We cannot help but be influenced, any more than we can help the fact that others will be influenced by us.

The instruction manual for using this hypnotic language pattern begins sequentially with: (a) First, determine boundaries, (b) Second, observe instances when your hypnotic subject uses words like: should, shouldn't, must, mustn't, can, can't, etc. (all modal operators of necessity or possibility), (c) Third, use their language against them when the opportunity arises—for example, if the subject has stated that they should think about your offer before making a decision, and later it they state that did something without thinking about it, you can ask them how that situation worked out for them, and when they say, "Excellently!" you can then use that to reframe their argument about waiting to make a decision with your offer, stating something like: "If you <u>can</u> make a decision without thinking about it and get an excellent result, what do you think <u>will</u> happen if you think you '<u>should</u>' wait to make a decision? <u>Shouldn't</u> you just *make a decision now*, so you get an *excellent* result?"

Notice in this example, how the modal operators are underlined, how an embedded command is italicized, and how I've italicized the 'power words' that the subject tends to lean on; namely, "Excellently/Excellent."

Until now I haven't mentioned it, yet you must get into a habit of reiterating and using words that your hypnotic subject tends to lean on, as these words are important to them, and have positive associations, which not only help you build much greater rapport with the subject, they also anchor a positive emotion with an action you want them to take: In this case it is to *'make a decision now'*.

Perhaps you didn't notice it, but I used a modal operator of necessity in the above paragraph on you, the reader. I stated emphatically: "...you <u>must</u> *get into a habit* of reiterating and using words that your hypnotic subject tends to lean on..." Notice how you focus on the 'must' part of the sentence; yet, the embedded command 'get into a habit' goes more or less under the radar of your conscious mind. I have done this to illustrate 'how' you can use the Modal Operator Hypnotic Language Pattern to get a result you want.

How Else This Hypnotic Language Pattern Might Be Utilized Applicably In Other Useful Contexts

The key ingredient to utilizing the power of the Modal Operator Pattern is being able to read and understand someone's limits and use them advantageously. This can be done on both small and large scales. Politicians commonly use this pattern by appealing to a particular group's principal beliefs and ideas. They appear to align themselves to those same principles in order to gain support. Counselors also use this pattern to help clients willingly make changes and alter their mindset. They will ask questions in order to figure out what the desired result is and encourage the patient to look inward at themselves in order to recognize flaws, senselessness, or unnecessary tendencies that are preventing personal growth.

Final Purport

Modal Operators Patterns are used by appealing to a person's sense of necessity. Getting them to question how necessary something is or should be is the first step in persuading or suggesting they place importance on something else or broaden their focus. It is a convenient pattern because everyone feels obligated to something, but it can be difficult for the simple fact that not everyone feels obligated about the same things. In order to have a persuasive impact, the "big picture" must be the same for the both parties.

Action Steps

There is a principle someone taught me once, which they labeled the 'Law of Action'. It basically claims, that you can learn anything, be the most brilliant mind, but if you don't take what you know and put it into action, it's worthless. I'm guilty of this, so let me be first to raise my own hand.

For years I learned information from reading books, attending seminars, being a student (I have multiple degrees), and still I remained broke, and sometimes penniless.

Then I read a book, and got inspired to take action, and start sharing all this knowledge with others. I took a job as a sales trainer, and taught others what I knew, and not surprisingly the company I contracted to prospered abundantly. Then I started my own company, and began experiencing huge results. Today, I have a new habit: I take what I learn and teach it to others, for profit of course, and I love it. Action is my best friend, and was the missing ingredient in my life. Since I learned this law, I have never looked back, and my life has become a lot more meaningful, and more richly rewarded.

All of this being said, I encourage you to do the following action steps; not because I want to waste your time, but because I want you to have the results you want. You should maximize the value of this book, and earn an exponential return on your investment, my opinion anyway!

I. Take this pattern and use it on ten people, and observe critically the response you're given by the other person. Watch for their physiology, their voice tonality, and what they actually say. More important usually is not what is said, but 'how' it's said. The word 'how' relates to energy or quality. When someone's response is congruently aligned with their physiology they are usually telling the truth, and resistance is lessened or non-existent. If someone tells you what you want to hear, but their physiology isn't congruently aligned, assume the opposite.

II. Write a journal entry on your experiences using this 'exact' hypnotic language pattern. Note whether or not you got closer to your desired

outcome, or further away. Also note if the person complied and took action or not.

III.   Make it a point to memorize this hypnotic language pattern now. The easiest way to do this is to use it on as many people as you can. Make it a part of your everyday language. Sooner or later you'll be using it unconsciously, and when you do you'll know that you're exactly where you need to be.

IV.   Teach this hypnotic language pattern to a friend or family member and explain what you've learned in this chapter to them. Perhaps this person will be someone whom you can feed patterns back and forth off of, to help you master these 25 hypnotic language patterns sooner.

V.   Get a 3x5 index card, and cut it in half vertically; namely, making two 'almost square' rectangles, and write this hypnotic language pattern on the front side. Below the pattern, make an abridged note to help you remember what contexts you should use the pattern in.

CHAPTER 10

Hypnotic Language Pattern Nine of Twenty-Five

> *HYPNOTIC LANGUAGE PATTERN*
>
> *WOULD YOU LIKE ___ OR ___?*

In the past years, hypnotic language patterns have become increasingly more popular than ever with thousands of people starting to subscribe to different channels and blog posts to learn about the usage and application of different patterns. Although people are now well-aware of the secrets of them, some patterns are still so compelling and work almost all the time when using by clever speakers. One basic pattern for beginners to learn is "Would you like ... A or B?" This is arguably one of the first hypnotic language patterns discovered by researchers, but it never seems too outdated to use.

Why Is This Hypnotic Language Pattern Important To Learn

The pattern is formulated as "Would you like ... A or B?" in which, A and B are the two options that the speaker allows the listener to choose from. An example of it is "Would you like to buy this product, the white one or the blue one?" The reason this pattern is so important is that it is very powerful, and carries within itself all the secrets of the art of persuasion. It is likely to be the first one people learn when they take any lesson about hypnotic language pattern. "Would you like ... A or B?" unconsciously makes the listener bypass the actual action that the speaker wants to him to take, and shifts his attention to deciding between A or B. For example in the previous question, the speaker effectively makes it appear that the listener has two choices "the white one or the blue one", while in fact it does not matter which one they choose. What matters to the speaker is that by starting to think about "the white one or the blue one", he implicitly agrees to buy the product.

What You Need To Know About This Hypnotic Language Pattern

The essence of this pattern is quite simple, but it takes some preparation and practice to be applied successfully.

The key to success of this is to make the two options A and B so attractive to the listener that they fascinate the listener and capture their full interest. This strategy works best when you place it at the end of your presentation, after you convincingly deliver the speech and want to urge your listener to take actions. Another thing you should keep in mind is to prepare your A and B options carefully in advance so that if the listener has more follow-up questions, you can answer them persuasively.

How To Use This Hypnotic Language Pattern To Effectively Win People Over To Your Persuasions

As mentioned earlier, "Would you like ... A or B?" pattern helps you to win people by making you look flexible and the listener to feel like they have choices. Psychologists have proved that people prefer to have options, and the more options, the better. They also tend to dislike being forced to do something. With this pattern, you can successfully hide your order, and induce them to think about your offers instead of your command. However, since people become smarter than before, when you use this pattern, you should know how to say it in a most congruent way and avoid all expressions giving hints to your real intention.

How Else This Hypnotic Language Pattern Might Be Utilized Applicably In Other Useful Contexts

The most common context to apply this pattern is in sales pitch to close the deal with the potential customers. However, you can also apply it to almost all other contexts providing that you can come up with the two convenient options for the listener to choose from. Parents can use it to ask their children to help with house chores by saying something like "What would you like to help me with, cleaning the house or doing your laundry?". When working in a team, you can use it to assign different tasks to your co-workers, without appearing bossy and authoritarian.

Final Purport

In sum, the "Would you like ... A or B?" pattern is a very powerful one that gives listeners little opportunities for resistance. In order to achieve a greater impact on a more critical audience, you can practice combining it with other hypnotic language patterns. In fact, the more you repeat your choices, the less resistant people are to making a decisions, as they become primed enough to not think anything about it.

Action Steps

There is a principle someone taught me once, which they labeled the 'Law of Action'. It basically claims, that you can learn anything, be the most brilliant mind, but if you don't take what you know and put it into action, it's worthless. I'm guilty of this, so let me be first to raise my own hand.

For years I learned information from reading books, attending seminars, being a student (I have multiple degrees), and still I remained broke, and sometimes penniless.

Then I read a book, and got inspired to take action, and start sharing all this knowledge with others. I took a job as a sales trainer, and taught others what I knew, and not surprisingly the company I contracted to prospered abundantly. Then I started my own company, and began experiencing huge results. Today, I have a new habit: I take what I learn and teach it to others, for profit of course, and I love it. Action is my best friend, and was the missing ingredient in my life. Since I learned this law, I have never looked back, and my life has become a lot more meaningful, and more richly rewarded.

All of this being said, I encourage you to do the following action steps; not because I want to waste your time, but because I want you to have the results you want. You should maximize the value of this book, and earn an exponential return on your investment, my opinion anyway!

I.   Take this pattern and use it on ten people, and observe critically the response you're given by the other person. Watch for their physiology, their voice tonality, and what they actually say. More important usually is not what is said, but 'how' it's said. The word 'how' relates to energy or quality. When someone's response is congruently aligned with their physiology they are usually telling the truth, and resistance is lessened or non-existent. If someone tells you what you want to hear, but their physiology isn't congruently aligned, assume the opposite.

II. Write a journal entry on your experiences using this 'exact' hypnotic language pattern. Note whether or not you got closer to your desired outcome, or further away. Also note if the person complied and took action or not.

III. Make it a point to memorize this hypnotic language pattern now. The easiest way to do this is to use it on as many people as you can. Make it a part of your everyday language. Sooner or later you'll be using it unconsciously, and when you do you'll know that you're exactly where you need to be.

IV. Teach this hypnotic language pattern to a friend or family member and explain what you've learned in this chapter to them. Perhaps

this person will be someone whom you can feed patterns back and forth off of, to help you master these 25 hypnotic language patterns sooner.

V. Get a 3x5 index card, and cut it in half vertically; namely, making two 'almost square' rectangles, and write this hypnotic language pattern on the front side. Below the pattern, make an abridged note to help you remember what contexts you should use the pattern in.

CHAPTER 11

Hypnotic Language Pattern Ten of Twenty-Five

HYPNOTIC LANGUAGE PATTERN

LINGUISTIC PRESUPPOSITION PATTERNS ONE

In this chapter I'm going to be sharing with you an amazing hypnotic language pattern that is going to help you communicate much more hypnotically. First I'm going to share with you 'why' this is important, and talk about how secretive and covert using presuppositions can be, while sharing how they can be used to increase your influence over others. Then I'm going to be sharing with you 'what' you need to know about this particular 'hypnotic language pattern', specifically covering how presuppositions can be used to indirectly plant ideas into someone's mind. Next

I'm going to literally explain to you 'how' you can use this hypnotic language patter to achieve the result of influencing other people to adopt your persuasions, while also going over how presuppositions can be used effectively to decrease resistance. Finally, I'm going to explore with you some other ways this hypnotic language pattern might actually help you indirectly excel in sales and see that the possible uses and benefits from using this pattern are endless.

By the time you are done reading this chapter, you will know more than a little about Hypnotic Presuppositions, and you will immediately find ways to apply them, easily. By the way, this introduction has been a presupposition!

Why Is This Hypnotic Language Pattern Important To Learn

So, you may be asking yourself, why it is important to learn about hypnotic presuppositions. Hypnotic presuppositions are extremely effective language patterns that are ever-present, and all of us use them unconsciously at times. Learning to consciously use presuppositions will dramatically improve the quality of your communication with others, and skillful use will allow you to gently influence others when the need arises. I am sure you can see the tremendous value of this simple yet little used technology. By learning about presuppositions and how you can apply them, and what other applications you might think up on your own where they will work for your purposes, you become a better persuasive communicator, while also a more aware and critical orator.

What You Need To Know About This Hypnotic Language Pattern

Now, what are some of the things you need to know about presuppositions? First of all, presuppositions, when properly used, introduce ideas unconsciously into the mind. For example, if I say "Football is the most rigorous of all sports", the statement presupposes the existence of other sports. Your mind automatically makes connections that call to mind other sports, to make sense out of the statement. I'm sure you didn't stop and say, "There are no other sports"; your mind automatically accepted that part of the statement. That is how presuppositions work.

You also need to know some basic types of presuppositions. Let's talk about Complex Presuppositions. Complex Presuppositions deal with more than just the existence of something, and there are many types of them. Let's discuss a few of them. Comparative Presuppositions can be conditional. They follow an "If _ then_" pattern. For example you could say, "If you work out, then you will improve your fitness". This presupposed that working out is beneficial. Subordinate Clauses of Time begin with words like after, before, during, while, and the like. An example would be "Would you like to_ while I_?" This causes attention to be directed to the first part of the statement, presupposing the second part. Even simple questions can be Complex Presuppositions. For example, if I ask, "Who spilled this milk?" this presupposes that some-one in fact spilled some milk. Unless of course I'm using it metaphorically, in which case I'm using quite another ele-ment of hypnotic communication—one that crosses the line into Hypnotic Storytelling. Check Amazon.com as I have another excellent book on that subject. Or visit: www.indirectknowledge.com as you can pick up a copy there as well.

How To Use This Hypnotic Language Pattern To Effectively Win People Over To Your Persuasions

Accordingly, how can we use presuppositions to real-istically persuade others? Oftentimes when we are con-versing with others, we may naively use patterns of speech which may express the wrong idea, or even make others resistant to an idea we are attempting to discuss. We therefore need to be conscious of the patterns we use so that others understand what we are trying to get across. People tend to have ingrained world views and senti-ments, but just by thinking about how you want to phrase something before you say it, and using these simple pat-terns, you can bypass much of this natural resistance.

How Else This Hypnotic Language Pattern Might Be Utilized Applicably In Other Useful Contexts

These patterns can be valuable in any sphere of human contact. At home, in the workplace, while giving a speech or a presentation, on a sales call. The options in truth are endless. Only your imagination will limit your options for application.

When you think about all the ways you can apply presuppositions to your everyday conversations, you realize all the ways you haven't yet considered, don't you. And, by the way, the previous sentence—it too was a presupposition. I was assuming that you would be thinking about all the ways you could apply presuppositions to your repertoire of persuasion situations.

Final Purport

In this chapter I shared with you an astonishing hypnotic language pattern. I explained that it would help you change minds easily and simply. I then shared with you 'why' you should commit to learning and using this hypnotic language pattern; emphasizing how presuppositions will increase your range of communication skills. Then I shared everything you needed to know about the hypnotic language pattern; namely: (a) to introduce ideas, (b) make believable assumptions, and (c) get your hypnotic subject to accept anything you say as the truth. After explaining what you needed to know, I explained step-by-step 'how' you can use this hypnotic language pattern to achieve the results you desire. Explicitly, I told you that step one meant becoming aware that people all the time use patterns of speech that convey the wrong idea; that step two you should start to become more critical and conscious of how you say what you say to determine the efficacy of it's impact on your hypnotic subject, and step three you needed to know how what you say will affect others, as it pertains to taking you closer to your desired outcome. Lastly, we explored some other ways this hypnotic language pattern might be useful. We took an interdisciplinary approach and decided that this hypnotic language pattern could be used in other contexts such as business, on the job, while delivering a persuasive speech, and so on. Used in these contexts the benefits one might realize could include: (a) more notoriety, (b) desired results, and (c) a greater range of communication skills.

As a result, just to recap on final time, on what have we have learned today: We have learned of the amazing power of to be able to consciously use Hypnotic Presuppositions. We have learned how they work, and how simple they are to apply. We now know of some basic types of presuppositions, such as the Complex form. We have knowledge of ways in which we can use them to effectively communicate with and influence others. Finally, we know that there is no limit to when and where they may be used.

Action Steps

There is a principle someone taught me once, which they labeled the 'Law of Action'. It basically claims, that you can learn anything, be the most brilliant mind, but if you don't take what you know and put it into action, it's worthless. I'm guilty of this, so let me be first to raise my own hand.

For years I learned information from reading books, attending seminars, being a student (I have multiple degrees), and still I remained broke, and sometimes penniless.

Then I read a book, and got inspired to take action, and start sharing all this knowledge with others. I took a job as a sales trainer, and taught others what I knew, and not surprisingly the company I contracted to prospered abundantly. Then I started my own company, and began experiencing huge results. Today, I have a new habit: I take what I learn and teach it to others, for profit of course, and I love it. Action is my best friend, and was the missing ingredient in my life. Since I learned this law, I have never looked back, and my life has become a lot more meaningful, and more richly rewarded.

All of this being said, I encourage you to do the following action steps; not because I want to waste your time, but because I want you to have the results you want. You should maximize the value of this book, and earn an exponential return on your investment, my opinion anyway!

I. Take this pattern and use it on ten people, and observe critically the response you're given by the other person. Watch for their physiology, their voice tonality, and what they actually say. More important usually is not what is said, but 'how' it's said. The word 'how' relates to energy or quality. When someone's response is congruently aligned with their physiology they are usually telling the truth, and resistance is lessened or non-existent. If someone tells you what you want to hear, but their physiology isn't congruently aligned, assume the opposite.

II. Write a journal entry on your experiences using this 'exact' hypnotic language pattern. Note whether or not you got closer to your desired outcome, or further away. Also note if the person complied and took action or not.

III. Make it a point to memorize this hypnotic language pattern now. The easiest way to do this is to use it on as many people as you can. Make it a part of your everyday language. Sooner or later you'll be using it unconsciously, and when you do you'll know that you're exactly where you need to be.

IV. Teach this hypnotic language pattern to a friend or family member and explain what you've learned in this chapter to them. Perhaps

this person will be someone whom you can feed patterns back and forth off of, to help you master these 25 hypnotic language patterns sooner.

V. Get a 3x5 index card, and cut it in half vertically; namely, making two 'almost square' rectangles, and write this hypnotic language pattern on the front side. Below the pattern, make an abridged note to help you remember what contexts you should use the pattern in.

CHAPTER 12

Hypnotic Language Pattern Eleven of Twenty-Five

HYPNOTIC LANGUAGE PATTERN

LINGUISTIC PRESUPPOSITION PATTERNS TWO

Language is by far one of the most complex modes of communication between two or more humans. Unlike other mammals in the animal kingdom, humans utilize the power of speech, which encompasses much more than just words, to communicate desires, emotions, fears and objectives. What makes language so effective is its ability to subconsciously affect its listeners. Hypnotic language patterns, also known as linguistic presuppositions, is a powerful tool capable of suggesting outcomes and navigating conversations - both external and internal. But what are these language patterns and how do they truly affect the world around us?

Why is This Hypnotic Language Pattern Important to Learn?

Have you ever wished you could navigate conversations toward a specific goal without the use of blatant linguistic techniques? Hypnotic language patterns work to influence conversations. Influence is among the most powerful tools within your communication toolbox. Through clear and understated language patterns, it's possible to influence decisions and opinions of listeners. While this has obvious benefits, those in a position of power or education professionals benefit from this linguistic technique as it demands attention and provides easier navigation toward an end goal.

What You Need To Know About This Hypnotic Language Pattern

Linguistic Presuppositions are fairly easy to understand; however, the depth of knowledge required to master this speaking skill is massive. On a foundational level, the most important thing you must know is hypnotic language patters are typically based in establishing the current physical action of listeners or readers and then suggestion the outcome.

For example, "The more you research about hypnotic language patterns the more you'll master its techniques to the point of true understanding." In this example, your current action is stated (the more you research about hypnotic language patterns), readers are actually researching. Following this current statement is the future outcome, "the more you'll master its techniques." Lastly, an uplifting goal is established, "...to the point of true understanding." Of course, formula is the most basic explanation of this technique. Nonetheless, if you master this skill then more advanced techniques are soon to follow.

How to use this hypnotic language pattern to effectively win people over to your persuasions

Winning people over through the power of this speaking technique is not learned overnight. That being said, begin practicing the aforementioned technique when speaking or writing to others. Maintain full control over the conversation by always acknowledging their current action or placement within your world, and then follow this statement with the true purpose of your conversation; however, keep the illusion of options to your conversational partner.

How Else This Hypnotic Language Pattern Might Be Utilized Applicably in Other Useful Contexts

The art of communication is invaluable in almost every aspect of life. Hypnotic language patterns are not only effective at influencing conversations, but also enhances how others view you. Speaking in such a manner is essential for job interviews or when dealing with prospective clients. Even in everyday interactions, such as in restaurants, linguistic presuppositions may alter interactions in a positive manner.

Final Purport

As you've read through this chapter, you've been introduced to the basic elements of hypnotic language patterns. While elementary in its scope of this subject, these foundational building blocks prepare your mind and teach you the necessary skills to begin altering how others hear and react to your words.

Action Steps

There is a principle someone taught me once, which they labeled the 'Law of Action'. It basically claims, that you can learn anything, be the most brilliant mind, but if you don't take what you know and put it into action, it's worthless. I'm guilty of this, so let me be first to raise my own hand.

For years I learned information from reading books, attending seminars, being a student (I have multiple degrees), and still I remained broke, and sometimes penniless.

Then I read a book, and got inspired to take action, and start sharing all this knowledge with others. I took a job as a sales trainer, and taught others what I knew, and not surprisingly the company I contracted to prospered abundantly. Then I started my own company, and began experiencing huge results. Today, I have a new habit: I take what I learn and teach it to others, for profit of course, and I love it. Action is my best friend, and was the missing ingredient in my life. Since I learned this law, I have never looked back, and my life has become a lot more meaningful, and more richly rewarded.

All of this being said, I encourage you to do the following action steps; not because I want to waste your time, but because I want you to have the results you want. You should maximize the value of this book, and earn an exponential return on your investment, my opinion anyway!

I. Take this pattern and use it on ten people, and observe critically the response you're given by the other person. Watch for their physiology, their voice tonality, and what they actually say. More important usually is not what is said, but 'how' it's said. The word 'how' relates to energy or quality. When someone's response is congruently aligned with their physiology they are

usually telling the truth, and resistance is lessened or non-existent. If someone tells you what you want to hear, but their physiology isn't congruently aligned, assume the opposite.

II.   Write a journal entry on your experiences using this 'exact' hypnotic language pattern. Note whether or not you got closer to your desired outcome, or further away. Also note if the person complied and took action or not.

III.   Make it a point to memorize this hypnotic language pattern now. The easiest way to do this is to use it on as many people as you can. Make it a part of your everyday language. Sooner or later you'll be using it unconsciously, and when you do you'll know that you're exactly where you need to be.

IV.   Teach this hypnotic language pattern to a friend or family member and explain what you've learned in this chapter to them. Perhaps this person will be someone whom you can feed patterns back and forth off of, to help you master these 25 hypnotic language patterns sooner.

V.   Get a 3x5 index card, and cut it in half vertically; namely, making two 'almost square' rectangles, and write this hypnotic language

pattern on the front side. Below the pattern, make an abridged note to help you remember what contexts you should use the pattern in.

CHAPTER 13

Hypnotic Language Pattern Twelve of Twenty-Five

HYPNOTIC LANGUAGE PATTERN

____SO YOU CAN___

In this chapter I'm going to be sharing with you an amazing hypnotic language pattern that is going to help you maximize the benefits from skillful use of interpersonal communication. First I'm going to share with you 'why' this is important and talk about the structure of our brains.

Then I'm going to be sharing with you 'what' you need to know about this particular 'hypnotic language pattern', specifically covering what is going on in different parts of our minds in different situations. Next I'm going to literally explain to you 'how' you can use this hypnotic language pattern to achieve increased effectiveness in business, sales, and interpersonal relationships of many kinds. Finally, I'm going to explore with you some other ways this hypnotic language pattern might actually help you indirectly find the kind of success you desire and deserve.

Why Is This Hypnotic Language Pattern Important To Learn

Human beings have come a long way in our development over the eons, but it did not happen all at once. Like many other creatures we developed slowly over time, and this applies to our brains as well. There are three well known areas of our brains that have distinct characteristics, and process information in different ways. Knowing this hypnotic language pattern will allow you to effectively communicate in the proper way with the part of the mind that you need to, and having this skill is of paramount importance for the kind of communication that can only be described as life changing.

What You Need To Know About This Hypnotic Language Pattern

First, let's talk about the " _so you can_ " pattern. It's called a presupposition. The first blank could contain an 'x', the second blank a 'y'. The 'x' is a call to action, and the 'y' is an advantage, a benefit, or both. Advantages are logical and benefits are emotional responses to stimuli.

Next, let's talk more about the parts of the brain. The first part I'd like to discuss is the reptilian brain. This was our first brain, and can be characterized by the "fight or flight" nature of it. A good example would be the feeling one gets when one finds oneself in a deserted parking lot late at night in a questionable neighborhood. That feeling you get in that situation is fight or flight. The second part of the brain I'd like to mention is the emotional brain, or limbic system. Some folks call this the unconscious, other folks call it the 'other' brain. This part of the brain is characterized by its emotional response to situations. The third part of the brain is the cortex, or conscious mind; this part controls logic, languages, and is what separates humans from other creatures. Therefore, effectively using the 'so you can' presupposition allows us to "speak" to the part of the mind that we need to get results.

How To Use This Hypnotic Language Pattern To Effectively Win People Over To Your Persuasions

Remember, the 'x' space in the 'so you can' pattern is a call to action, and the 'y' space is an advantage (logical) or a benefit (emotional).

Let's do an exercise and fill in those boxes. I could say "Buy this product -so you can- save money"; saving money is usually a logical response, so that would be an appeal to logic. Or, it could be "Buy this product-so you can- spend

time with your family"; that would be speaking emotionally to the limbic, unconscious mind. Very powerful.

How Else This Hypnotic Language Pattern Might Be Utilized Applicably in Other Useful Contexts

The separate parts of our minds have the same characteristics, in all situations. So the real answer is, this hypnotic language pattern is effective and applicable to just
about any context in which we wish to communicate with
and influence people effectively.

Final Purport

In this chapter I shared with you an astonishing hypnotic language pattern. I explained that it would help you
maximize benefits from skillful use of tools of communication. I then shared with you why you should commit to
learning and using this hypnotic language pattern; emphasizing the basic structure of our brains. Then I shared everything you needed to know about the hypnotic language
pattern; namely: the _so you can_ pattern. After explaining what you needed to know, I explained step-by-step
how you can use this hypnotic language pattern to achieve
the results you desire. Explicitly, I told you that step one
meant doing a call to action; that step two you should
name an advantage, and step three you needed to identify
a benefit. Lastly, we explored some other ways this hyp-

notic language pattern might be useful. We took an inter-disciplinary approach and decided that this hypnotic language pattern could be used in other contexts such as in the workplace, and in our personal relationships. Used in these contexts the benefits one might realize could include: (a) financial, (b) emotional, and (c) reaching our goals.

Action Steps

There is a principle someone taught me once, which they labeled the 'Law of Action'. It basically claims, that you can learn anything, be the most brilliant mind, but if you don't take what you know and put it into action, it's worthless. I'm guilty of this, so let me be first to raise my own hand.

For years I learned information from reading books, attending seminars, being a student (I have multiple degrees), and still I remained broke, and sometimes penniless.

Then I read a book, and got inspired to take action, and start sharing all this knowledge with others. I took a job as a sales trainer, and taught others what I knew, and not surprisingly the company I contracted to prospered abundantly. Then I started my own company, and began experiencing huge results. Today, I have a new habit: I take what I learn and teach it to others, for profit of course, and I love it. Action is my best friend, and was the missing ingredient in my life. Since I learned this law, I have never

looked back, and my life has become a lot more meaningful, and more richly rewarded.

All of this being said, I encourage you to do the following action steps; not because I want to waste your time,
but because I want you to have the results you want. You
should maximize the value of this book, and earn an exponential return on your investment, my opinion anyway!

I.   Take this pattern and use it on ten people, and
observe critically the response you're given by
the other person. Watch for their physiology,
their voice tonality, and what they actually say.
More important usually is not what is said, but
'how' it's said. The word 'how' relates to energy
or quality. When someone's response is congruently aligned with their physiology they are
usually telling the truth, and resistance is lessened or non-existent. If someone tells you what
you want to hear, but their physiology isn't
congruently aligned, assume the opposite.

II.   Write a journal entry on your experiences using this 'exact' hypnotic language pattern. Note
whether or not you got closer to your desired
outcome, or further away. Also note if the person complied and took action or not.

III.   Make it a point to memorize this hypnotic language pattern now. The easiest way to do this
is to use it on as many people as you can. Make

it a part of your everyday language. Sooner or later you'll be using it unconsciously, and when you do you'll know that you're exactly where you need to be.

IV.   Teach this hypnotic language pattern to a friend or family member and explain what you've learned in this chapter to them. Perhaps this person will be someone whom you can feed patterns back and forth off of, to help you master these 25 hypnotic language patterns sooner.

V.   Get a 3x5 index card, and cut it in half vertically; namely, making two 'almost square' rectangles, and write this hypnotic language pattern on the front side. Below the pattern, make an abridged note to help you remember what contexts you should use the pattern in.

CHAPTER 14

Hypnotic Language Pattern Thirteen of Twenty-Five

HYPNOTIC LANGUAGE PATTERN

YOU MAY HAVE ALREADY STARTED TO NOTICE ___

In this chapter I'm going to be sharing with you an amazing hypnotic language pattern that is going to help you sharpen your ability to influence others. First I'm going to share with you 'why' this is important and talk about how you can get folks to really extend themselves to aid you in going all out to help you achieve your goals, and also, importantly, to help them get what they really want.

Then I'm going to be sharing with you 'what' you need to know about this specific hypnotic language pattern, specifically covering facts about the human mind and brain which will make clear why this pattern works so well. Next I'm going to literally explain to you 'how' you can use this hypnotic language pattern to achieve the ability to speak to the natural parts of the human brain and mind that will enable you to bypass natural but unnecessary resistance to influence. Finally, I'm going to explore with you some other ways this hypnotic language pattern might actually help you indirectly do things you have only imagined that you can do.

Why Is This Hypnotic Language Pattern Important To Learn

Contrary to popular belief, the human mind is not a monolithic structure. The mind is actually comprised of distinct, separate parts. The first part we will discuss is the reptilian brain. This was the first brain structure that appeared, and is also known as the "flight or fight' part of the mind. When we find ourselves in unfamiliar and possibly dangerous situations, such as, let's say, walking down a dark alley in an unfamiliar city, this part of the brain initiates a 'fight or flight' response which I'm sure we've all experienced. The second part of the brain I'd like to discuss is the 'other brain', or, as some describe it, the unconscious or emotional mind. When humans are faced with a choice which involves a benefit, such as something which helps a family member, we engage our emotional brain. The third, and most modern, part of the brain which we will discuss is the cortex, or the conscious mind. This part of the mind is responsible for such things as logic, languages, and advantageous choices. When we make choices based on advantage, we are using this part of our brain.

What you need to know about this hypnotic language pattern

The most important thing about this, and indeed other, hypnotic language patterns, is the way in which they speak directly to the part of the brain/mind which we need to be speaking to at any given moment or in any given situation. When effectively using hypnotic language patterns, what we want to be doing is speaking directly, without natural resistance, to the limbic, unconscious part of the brain, and to a lesser extent to the advantageously thinking, cerebral cortex.

How To Use This Hypnotic Language Pattern To Effectively Win People Over To Your Persuasions

When you say something like "You may have already started to notice...<u>something or other</u>," your unconscious hypnotic mind is already starting to notice or think about the object of the sentence or situation, independent of anything else! The mind will automatically *take to heart* the first part of the statement unconsciously. Using language patterns of this type effectively bypasses the conscious critical mind. This kind of power should only be undertaken ethically, with your subjects' best interests in mind.

How Else This Hypnotic Language Pattern Might Be Utilized Applicably In Other Useful Contexts

The brain works the same way 365 days a year, 24/7 hours a day, and so these hypnotic language patterns will work at any time that the brain is working, in any situation. You can therefore infer that they can be applied to any instance where you want to influence someone to believe your persuasions, change their minds, and take some type of decisive action.

Even though these language patterns are indirect and artfully vague in nature, they still have a greater impact than direct commands (in most situational contexts). You'll decide for yourself how best to use them, as you use them more and more regularly.

Final Purport

In this chapter I shared with you an astonishing hypnotic language pattern. I explained that it would help you encourage folks to extend themselves to help you, and, all importantly, to help themselves in the process. I then shared with you 'why' you should commit to learning and using this hypnotic language pattern; emphasizing the basic structure of the human brain. Then I shared everything you needed to know about this hypnotic language pattern; namely:

I.   There are disparate parts to the brain,

II.   We need to speak directly to the limbic, i.e., unconscious part of the mind, and,

III.   We should also engage, when necessary, the conscious, advantageously thinking, cortex.

After explaining what you needed to know, I explained step-by-step 'how' you can use this hypnotic language pattern to achieve the results you desire. Explicitly, I told you that step one meant saying "You may have already started to notice <u>something or other</u>." That step two, assuming proper use of step one, the mind has already accepted the statement in step one, and step three it helps to offer an advantage to the cortex. Lastly, we explored some ways in which this hypnotic language pattern might be useful. We took an interdisciplinary approach and decided that this hypnotic language pattern might be useful in other contexts such as sales calls for instance. Used in these contexts the benefits one might realize could include familial, financial, and healthful profits.

Action Steps

There is a principle someone taught me once, which they labeled the 'Law of Action'. It basically claims, that you can learn anything, be the most brilliant mind, but if you don't take what you know and put it into action, it's worthless. I'm guilty of this, so let me be first to raise my own hand.

For years I learned information from reading books, attending seminars, being a student (I have multiple degrees), and still I remained broke, and sometimes penniless.

Then I read a book, and got inspired to take action, and start sharing all this knowledge with others. I took a job as a sales trainer, and taught others what I knew, and not surprisingly the company I contracted to prospered abundantly. Then I started my own company, and began experiencing huge results. Today, I have a new habit: I take what I learn and teach it to others, for profit of course, and I love it. Action is my best friend, and was the missing ingredient in my life. Since I learned this law, I have never looked back, and my life has become a lot more meaningful, and more richly rewarded.

All of this being said, I encourage you to do the following action steps; not because I want to waste your time, but because I want you to have the results you want. You should maximize the value of this book, and earn an exponential return on your investment, my opinion anyway!

I. Take this pattern and use it on ten people, and observe critically the response you're given by the other person. Watch for their physiology, their voice tonality, and what they actually say. More important usually is not what is said, but 'how' it's said. The word 'how' relates to energy or quality. When someone's response is congruently aligned with their physiology they are

usually telling the truth, and resistance is lessened or non-existent. If someone tells you what
you want to hear, but their physiology isn't
congruently aligned, assume the opposite.

II.   Write a journal entry on your experiences using this 'exact' hypnotic language pattern. Note
whether or not you got closer to your desired
outcome, or further away. Also note if the person complied and took action or not.

III.   Make it a point to memorize this hypnotic language pattern now. The easiest way to do this
is to use it on as many people as you can. Make
it a part of your everyday language. Sooner or
later you'll be using it unconsciously, and when
you do you'll know that you're exactly where
you need to be.

IV.   Teach this hypnotic language pattern to a
friend or family member and explain what
you've learned in this chapter to them. Perhaps
this person will be someone whom you can
feed patterns back and forth off of, to help you
master these 25 hypnotic language patterns
sooner.

V.   Get a 3x5 index card, and cut it in half vertically; namely, making two 'almost square' rectangles, and write this hypnotic language

pattern on the front side. Below the pattern, make an abridged note to help you remember what contexts you should use the pattern in.

CHAPTER 15

Hypnotic Language Pattern Fourteen of Twenty-Five

HYPNOTIC LANGUAGE PATTERN

WHEN YOU REALLY BEGIN TO ___ THEN ___.

In this chapter I'm going to be sharing with you an amazing hypnotic language pattern that is going to help you get what you want the smart way. First I'm going to share with you why this is important, and talk about getting your ideas and proposals across easily and smoothly. Then I'm going to be sharing with you what you need to know about this particular 'cause-effect' hypnotic language pattern, specifically covering how you can employ its use in everyday conversation. Next I'm going to literally explain to you how you can use this hypnotic language pattern to enhance your public speaking and communication skills. Finally, I'm going to explore with you some other ways this hypnotic language pattern might actually help you indirectly and help other people with their problems.

Why Is This Hypnotic Language Pattern Important To Learn

This hypnotic language pattern is important to learn because if properly used, it can help you to elegantly persuade others covertly. With this skill at hand, you can easily direct people's imaginations and this will lead them to act according to the picture you have already painted in their minds. Instead of your audience getting bored in the middle of your public address, the conversational hypnosis tool will help you improve your public speaking skills such that your audience will stay intrigued from beginning to end. So why not learn more about this particular hypnotic language pattern?

What You Need To Know About This Hypnotic Language Pattern

The various cause-effect hypnotic language patterns appeal to both one's logic and emotion. While it is considered smart to appeal to one's emotion more than their logic, appealing to both obviously comes with added advantages. When using the pattern 'When you really begin to … then …' you can easily manipulate learned behavior present in your listener's subconscious mind. By influencing one's subconscious mind, you can reach out and form bonds with even the most stubborn minds.

How To Use This Hypnotic Language Pattern To Effectively Win People Over To Your Persuasions

First, know the word sequence: "When you really begin to ... then ..." Secondly, prepare yourself. Since you cannot always control the time and place of your conversations, focus on what you can control- the subject of your conversation. In the beginning, you may need to sit down and come up with the right words that can apply to a particular situation. Fill in the blanks in the statement "when you really begin to ... then ..." with words that can apply to as many situations as possible. Continue practicing this technique so you eventually learn how to employ it effortlessly. Lastly, build rapport with your listener(s) by making sure every conversation is a dialogue. Ensure your listeners participate by allowing them to take lead in the discussion and sharing experiences that they can identify with.

How Else This Hypnotic Language Pattern Might Be Utilized Applicably In Other Useful Contexts

When not using this technique to further your own agenda, you may use it to positively influence other people's minds. This is how motivational speakers, therapists, life coaches and psychologists use hypnotic language patterns. In this way, you can help people with their problems. Learning to control other people's minds will also help you understand how you can exercise control over your own state of mind.

Final Purport

In this chapter I shared with you an astonishing hypnotic language pattern. I explained that it would help you improve your public speaking skills, help you communicate clearly and precisely with your listeners, direct people's imaginations hence their actions, and achieve your objectives faster and smarter. I then shared with you why you should commit to learning and using this hypnotic language pattern; emphasizing that since it appeals to both emotion and logic, it is one of the easiest hypnotic language patterns to use. Then I shared everything you needed to know about the hypnotic language pattern; namely: knowing the word sequence, preparing yourself, and lastly, building rapport with your listeners. Lastly, we explored some other ways this hypnotic language pattern might be useful. We took an interdisciplinary approach and decided that this hypnotic language pattern could be used in other contexts to realize benefits that include motivating others to overcome their problems and helping ourselves to control our own state of mind.

Action Steps

There is a principle someone taught me once, which they labeled the 'Law of Action'. It basically claims, that you can learn anything, be the most brilliant mind, but if you don't take what you know and put it into action, it's worthless. I'm guilty of this, so let me be first to raise my own hand.

For years I learned information from reading books, attending seminars, being a student (I have multiple degrees), and still I remained broke, and sometimes penniless.

Then I read a book, and got inspired to take action, and start sharing all this knowledge with others. I took a job as a sales trainer, and taught others what I knew, and not surprisingly the company I contracted to prospered abundantly. Then I started my own company, and began experiencing huge results. Today, I have a new habit: I take what I learn and teach it to others, for profit of course, and I love it. Action is my best friend, and was the missing ingredient in my life. Since I learned this law, I have never looked back, and my life has become a lot more meaningful, and more richly rewarded.

All of this being said, I encourage you to do the following action steps; not because I want to waste your time, but because I want you to have the results you want. You should maximize the value of this book, and earn an exponential return on your investment, my opinion anyway!

I.   Take this pattern and use it on ten people, and observe critically the response you're given by the other person. Watch for their physiology, their voice tonality, and what they actually say. More important usually is not what is said, but 'how' it's said. The word 'how' relates to energy or quality. When someone's response is congruently aligned with their physiology they are usually telling the truth, and resistance is lessened or non-existent. If someone tells you what you want to hear, but their physiology isn't congruently aligned, assume the opposite.

II.   Write a journal entry on your experiences using this 'exact' hypnotic language pattern. Note whether or not you got closer to your desired outcome, or further away. Also note if the person complied and took action or not.

III. Make it a point to memorize this hypnotic language pattern now. The easiest way to do this is to use it on as many people as you can. Make it a part of your everyday language. Sooner or later you'll be using it unconsciously, and when you do you'll know that you're exactly where you need to be.

IV.   Teach this hypnotic language pattern to a friend or family member and explain what you've learned in this chapter to them. Perhaps this person will be someone whom you can feed patterns back and forth off of, to help you master these 25 hypnotic language patterns sooner.

V.   Get a 3x5 index card, and cut it in half vertically; namely, making two 'almost square' rectangles, and write this hypnotic language pattern on the front side. Below the pattern, make an abridged note to help you remember what contexts you should use the pattern in.

CHAPTER 16

Hypnotic Language Pattern Fifteen of Twenty-Five

HYPNOTIC LANGUAGE PATTERN

A PERSON COULD ___

In this chapter I'm going to be sharing with you an amazing hypnotic language pattern that is going to help you influence other people easily and get things done the way you want them to. First I'm going to share with you 'why' this is important, and talk about the significance of this hypnotic language pattern in day to day life. Then I'm going to be sharing with you 'what' you need to know about this particular 'hypnotic language pattern', specifically covering the kind of tone, sentence structure, and words you should use. Next I'm going to literally explain to you 'how' you can use this hypnotic language patter to achieve the power of persuasion and ethically controlling the mind of your listener. Finally, I'm going to explore with you some other ways this hypnotic language pattern might actually help you indirectly do the things you want to do, such as influence your customers to buy more.

Why Is This Hypnotic Language Pattern Important To Learn

This hypnotic language pattern carries with it a large number of benefits, which makes it a very important language pattern to learn and memorize. A person could, by learning this pattern, be able to influence the people around them easily and convince them to agree with you more easily. You can make things run the way you want them to, and this would just be the beginning.

What You Need To Know About This Hypnotic Language Pattern

There are several things you need to know about this hypnotic language pattern, such as: what should be your voice inflection in different situations, how should you use your tone, how should you place emphasis on your words, and most of all; you must realize the impact your words have on the listener. You must choose your words carefully, deliver them in the right tone, place the right amount of emphasis on the right word, and empathize with the listener to understand the influence of your words. For example, when you start your sentence with the phrase "A person could…" the listener applies the situation of the person to himself. For example, when you say "a person could be highly successful in this business", the listener would assume himself as the person. Thus, by structuring your language pattern correctly, you can directly influence the person you communicate to.

How To Use This Hypnotic Language Pattern To Effectively Win People Over To Your Persuasions

Hypnotic language patterns can be used effective to persuade others by ensuring that you use the right sentence, in the right manner; at the right time. At all times, you must keep in mind that each and every word you deliver and in the manner you deliver it is being absorbed by the other person's subconscious and it is translating those words into visions. By keeping this in mind, you may use sentence structures that create subconscious visions in the mind of the listener which may amplify your argument. This way, you can easily win over another person in your persuasion.

How Else This Hypnotic Language Pattern Might Be Utilized Applicably In Other Useful Contexts

Imagine the significance of this attribute in bargaining and negotiations. You could get your favorite things at the prices you want. You can reach the consensus that you desire by influencing the person in front of you very easily. You can convince your customers to buy more from you In addition to that, you can become a great motivator by helping people break their 'auto-pilot' routines and reclaim the passions that they have left abandoned while trying to fit into society.

Final Purport

In this chapter I shared with you an astonishing hypnotic language pattern. I explained that it would help you acquire the power of persuasion which can be used in influencing customers, colleagues, and in winning arguments in negotiations. I then shared with you 'why' you should commit to learning and using this hypnotic language pattern; emphasizing its significance in day to day life and how you can get things done easily. Then I shared everything you needed to know about the hypnotic language pattern; namely: voice inflection, sentence structures, and tones. After explaining what you needed to know, I explained step-by-step 'how' you can use this hypnotic language pattern to achieve the results you desire. Explicitly, I told you that step one meant using the right sentence at the right time; that step two you should empathize with the listener and understand the impact of your words, and step three you needed to deliver the right words that invoked the right visions in the listener's subconscious. Lastly, we explored some other ways this hypnotic language pattern might be useful. We took an interdisciplinary approach and decided that this hypnotic language pattern could be used in other contexts such as bargaining and negotiation, and influencing customers. Used in these contexts the benefits one might realize could include: financial savings, achieving the desired goals efficiently, and growth in business.

Action Steps

There is a principle someone taught me once, which they labeled the 'Law of Action'. It basically claims, that you can learn anything, be the most brilliant mind, but if you don't take what you know and put it into action, it's worthless. I'm guilty of this, so let me be first to raise my own hand.

For years I learned information from reading books, attending seminars, being a student (I have multiple degrees), and still I remained broke, and sometimes penniless.

Then I read a book, and got inspired to take action, and start sharing all this knowledge with others. I took a job as a sales trainer, and taught others what I knew, and not surprisingly the company I contracted to prospered abundantly. Then I started my own company, and began experiencing huge results. Today, I have a new habit: I take what I learn and teach it to others, for profit of course, and I love it. Action is my best friend, and was the missing ingredient in my life. Since I learned this law, I have never looked back, and my life has become a lot more meaningful, and more richly rewarded.

All of this being said, I encourage you to do the following action steps; not because I want to waste your time, but because I want you to have the results you want. You should maximize the value of this book, and earn an exponential return on your investment, my opinion anyway!

I.   Take this pattern and use it on ten people, and observe critically the response you're given by the other person. Watch for their physiology, their voice tonality, and what they actually say. More important usually is not what is said, but 'how' it's said. The word 'how' relates to energy or quality. When someone's response is congruently aligned with their physiology they are usually telling the truth, and resistance is lessened or non-existent. If someone tells you what you want to hear, but their physiology isn't congruently aligned, assume the opposite.

II. Write a journal entry on your experiences using this 'exact' hypnotic language pattern. Note whether or not you got closer to your desired outcome, or further away. Also note if the person complied and took action or not.

III. Make it a point to memorize this hypnotic language pattern now. The easiest way to do this is to use it on as many people as you can. Make it a part of your everyday language. Sooner or later you'll be using it unconsciously, and when

you do you'll know that you're exactly where
you need to be.

IV.   Teach this hypnotic language pattern to a
friend or family member and explain what
you've learned in this chapter to them. Perhaps
this person will be someone whom you can
feed patterns back and forth off of, to help you
master these 25 hypnotic language patterns
sooner.

V.   Get a 3x5 index card, and cut it in half vertically; namely, making two 'almost square' rectangles, and write this hypnotic language
pattern on the front side. Below the pattern,
make an abridged note to help you remember
what contexts you should use the pattern in.

CHAPTER 17

Hypnotic Language Pattern Sixteen of Twenty-Five

HYPNOTIC LANGUAGE PATTERN

SIMPLE DELETION PATTERNS

NLP or Neural-Linguistic Programming is a form of indirect hypnosis which utilizes the voice in order to persuade the mind and influence the subconscious. It is broken down into a number of smaller methods called Hypnotic Language Patterns and referred to as The Milton Model. We will be exploring one of these methods called Simple Deletions. This chapter will explain the importance of Simple Deletions and why they are a relevant Hypnotic Language Pattern. It will also inform the reader about important facts and details regarding Simple Deletions and how and when to use them. Finally, the chapter will explore other instances or situations where this particular pattern may be useful and beneficial.

Why Is This Hypnotic Language Pattern Important To Learn

The Simple Deletions Hypnotic Language Pattern is important for the simple fact that it causes questions which gives a significant amount of power to the person who has the answers. Like its' name implies, Simple Deletions simply leave facts, meanings or descriptions unspoken or unfinished. This causes the other party to want to figure out what is missing from the story. It holds their attention and makes them want more information.

What You Need To Know About This Hypnotic Language Pattern

Although Simple Deletions can draw positive attention, they can also lead to misunderstandings. Leaving information out opens the door to "mind reading" attempts which can waste time and cause unnecessary problems. If employing this particular pattern, one must be certain to choose the deleted details wisely and with caution. Capturing a person's attention is no small task, but keeping it is even more difficult. If they become too frustrated by trying to fill in the information that is missing, they will become indifferent and lose interest.

How To Use This Hypnotic Language Pattern To Effectively Win People Over To Your Persuasions

Using Simple Deletions correctly and effectively can encourage others to listen and pay attention more diligently. Since the listener will have to fill in the missing information themselves, they will naturally work harder to concentrate in order to do so. For this reason all you have to do is simply deliver any type of phrase or sentence with the meaning, facts, or any clear description left out—forcing the subjects to make their own meaning and give more reference to what is important to them, which can in return help you persuade them more effectively.

How Else This Hypnotic Language Pattern Might Be Utilized Applicably In Other Useful Contexts

Simple Deletions are used much more than most people realize. Most marketing and advertising executives spend countless hours and millions of dollars trying to find ways to make their customers want more of what their company or its' affiliates are offering. They are extremely popular on television and most other methods of promoting products, such as magazine ads and book or movie reviews.

Final Purport

In an era in which most people will put an extremely large amount of trust in what others say, using the Simple Deletion Pattern can give its' user the ability to have crowds hanging onto every word and eager to find out what is coming next. While this may be beneficial and garner a huge following, it can also be quite dangerous. There is an extremely fine line between keeping someone's attention and causing them to become indifferent. Being able to recognize a Simple Deletion Hypnotic Language Pattern enables a person to hold attention, but also recognize and avoid if necessary. It is an extremely useful pattern to utilize when done correctly.

Action Steps

There is a principle someone taught me once, which they labeled the 'Law of Action'. It basically claims, that you can learn anything, be the most brilliant mind, but if you don't take what you know and put it into action, it's worthless. I'm guilty of this, so let me be first to raise my own hand.

For years I learned information from reading books, attending seminars, being a student (I have multiple degrees), and still I remained broke, and sometimes penniless.

Then I read a book, and got inspired to take action, and start sharing all this knowledge with others. I took a job as a sales trainer, and taught others what I knew, and not

surprisingly the company I contracted to prospered abundantly. Then I started my own company, and began experiencing huge results. Today, I have a new habit: I take what I learn and teach it to others, for profit of course, and I love it. Action is my best friend, and was the missing ingredient in my life. Since I learned this law, I have never looked back, and my life has become a lot more meaningful, and more richly rewarded.

All of this being said, I encourage you to do the following action steps; not because I want to waste your time, but because I want you to have the results you want. You should maximize the value of this book, and earn an exponential return on your investment, my opinion anyway!

I.   Take this pattern and use it on ten people, and observe critically the response you're given by the other person. Watch for their physiology, their voice tonality, and what they actually say. More important usually is not what is said, but 'how' it's said. The word 'how' relates to energy or quality. When someone's response is congruently aligned with their physiology they are usually telling the truth, and resistance is lessened or non-existent. If someone tells you what you want to hear, but their physiology isn't congruently aligned, assume the opposite.

II.   Write a journal entry on your experiences using this 'exact' hypnotic language pattern. Note whether or not you got closer to your desired

outcome, or further away. Also note if the person complied and took action or not.

III.   Make it a point to memorize this hypnotic language pattern now. The easiest way to do this is to use it on as many people as you can. Make it a part of your everyday language. Sooner or later you'll be using it unconsciously, and when you do you'll know that you're exactly where you need to be.

IV.   Teach this hypnotic language pattern to a friend or family member and explain what you've learned in this chapter to them. Perhaps this person will be someone whom you can feed patterns back and forth off of, to help you master these 25 hypnotic language patterns sooner.

V.   Get a 3x5 index card, and cut it in half vertically; namely, making two 'almost square' rectangles, and write this hypnotic language pattern on the front side. Below the pattern, make an abridged note to help you remember what contexts you should use the pattern in.

CHAPTER 18

Hypnotic Language Pattern Seventeen of Twenty-Five

HYPNOTIC LANGUAGE PATTERN

WHAT HAPPENS WHEN YOU ___

In this chapter I'm going to be sharing with you an amazing hypnotic language pattern that is going to help you achieve effortless influence in a myriad of situations as well as upgrade your communications skills. First I'm going to share with you 'why' this is important, and talk about the structure of the human brain. Then I'm going to share with you 'what' you need to know about this specific hypnotic language pattern, specifically covering things like advantages and benefits. Next I'm going to literally explain to you how you can use this hypnotic language pattern to achieve greater success in business, relationships, etc. Finally, I'm going to explore with you some other ways this hypnotic language pattern might actually help you indirectly do more to achieve your goals then you thought possible.

Why Is This Hypnotic Language Pattern Important To Learn

The human brain is an amazing object, but it took a while to assume its current form. Our earliest brain was the reptilian brain, and it holds sway over fight of flight responses which we experience in threatening situations. The next component to come along was our emotional, limbic or unconscious brain. This part of the brain is responsible for emotional responses to our environment. The last piece of the brain is the cortex, or the logical brain. This part of the brain is where your consciousness resides, and controls language and logic. All this is important to know because skillful use of this hypnotic language pattern will allow you to speak directly the part of the mind that you need to.

What You Need To Know About This Hypnotic Language Pattern

When you properly use the 'What happens when you___' hypnotic language pattern, you will gain access to the limbic, emotional part of the brain. This is the part of the brain that is engaged when we see the benefit in a situation, as opposed to the cortex which is engaged when we see an advantage. When you say something like "What happens when you imagine yourself retiring a wealthy person in three years", to find out what happens a person will need to access the part of the mind which is responsible for seeing benefits, essentially giving the person who used the hypnotic language pattern direct access to the unconscious. Very strong medicine.

How To Use This Hypnotic Language Pattern To Effectively Win People Over To Your Persuasions

Sometimes the best way to persuade someone is to allow them to persuade themselves, and this is where this pattern really comes into its own. Simply pose the question and fill the blank with anything you would like them to think about or imagine, and as they access their emotional mind the work is automatically being done for you.

How Else This Hypnotic Language Pattern Might Be Utilized Applicably In Other Useful Contexts

Given that the human mind is always 'on', so to speak, and works the same way all the time, this pattern is useful always, and all the time. I think this is one of the reasons it's one of my favorites. In order to answer the question the subject has to, i.e. is forced to, do a trans-derivational search for meaning and must consider an outcome. This consideration is what helps them sell themselves on your idea; namely, because when they are thinking about your idea, they are not thinking contrarian thoughts—helping you control the conversation and sell your idea to them.

Final Purport

In this chapter I shared with you an astonishing hypnotic language pattern. I explained that it would help you achieve effortless influence and heightened communication skills. I then shared with you 'why' you should commit to learning and using this hypnotic language pattern; emphasizing brain structure and function. Then I shared everything you need to know about this hypnotic language pattern; namely how to use it to speak directly to the limbic, unconscious mind. After explaining what you needed to know, I explained step by step 'how' you can use this hypnotic language pattern to achieve the results you desire. Explicitly, I told you that step one meant understanding that sometimes it's best to let others convince themselves; that step two you should ask the question in the pattern format; and step three you needed to fill in the blank with whatever you want their unconscious mind to think about. Lastly, we explored some other ways this hypnotic language pattern might be useful. We took an interdisciplinary approach and decided that this hypnotic language pattern could be used in other contexts such as at home, work, on a sales call, or in virtually any situation.

Used in these contexts, the benefits one might realize could include: social, financial, affective, and overall effectual results that help you change minds, win, and get rich.

Action Steps

There is a principle someone taught me once, which they labeled the 'Law of Action'. It basically claims, that you can learn anything, be the most brilliant mind, but if you don't take what you know and put it into action, it's worthless. I'm guilty of this, so let me be first to raise my own hand.

For years I learned information from reading books, attending seminars, being a student (I have multiple degrees), and still I remained broke, and sometimes penniless.

Then I read a book, and got inspired to take action, and start sharing all this knowledge with others. I took a job as a sales trainer, and taught others what I knew, and not surprisingly the company I contracted to prospered abundantly. Then I started my own company, and began experiencing huge results. Today, I have a new habit: I take what I learn and teach it to others, for profit of course, and I love it. Action is my best friend, and was the missing ingredient in my life. Since I learned this law, I have never looked back, and my life has become a lot more meaningful, and more richly rewarded.

All of this being said, I encourage you to do the following action steps; not because I want to waste your time, but because I want you to have the results you want. You should maximize the value of this book, and earn an exponential return on your investment, my opinion anyway!

I. Take this pattern and use it on ten people, and observe critically the response you're given by the other person. Watch for their physiology, their voice tonality, and what they actually say. More important usually is not what is said, but 'how' it's said. The word 'how' relates to energy or quality. When someone's response is congruently aligned with their physiology they are usually telling the truth, and resistance is lessened or non-existent. If someone tells you what you want to hear, but their physiology isn't congruently aligned, assume the opposite.

II. Write a journal entry on your experiences using this 'exact' hypnotic language pattern. Note whether or not you got closer to your desired outcome, or further away. Also note if the person complied and took action or not.

III. Make it a point to memorize this hypnotic language pattern now. The easiest way to do this is to use it on as many people as you can. Make it a part of your everyday language. Sooner or later you'll be using it unconsciously, and when you do you'll know that you're exactly where you need to be.

IV.   Teach this hypnotic language pattern to a friend or family member and explain what you've learned in this chapter to them. Perhaps this person will be someone whom you can feed patterns back and forth off of, to help you master these 25 hypnotic language patterns sooner.

V.   Get a 3x5 index card, and cut it in half vertically; namely, making two 'almost square' rectangles, and write this hypnotic language pattern on the front side. Below the pattern, make an abridged note to help you remember what contexts you should use the pattern in.

CHAPTER 19

Hypnotic Language Pattern Eighteen of Twenty-Five

HYPNOTIC LANGUAGE PATTERN

HOW WOULD YOU FEEL ___

In this chapter I'm going to be sharing with you an amazing hypnotic language pattern that is going to help you make people more receptive to you in what you are trying to persuade them about. First I'm going to share with you 'why' this is important, and talk about how and what makes it an effective persuasion technique. Then I'm going to be sharing with you 'what' you need to know about this particular 'hypnotic language pattern', specifically covering how it works to make people more receptive to what you are talking to them about. Next I'm going to literally explain to you 'how' you can use this hypnotic language pattern to achieve the results you want. Finally, I'm going to explore with you some other ways this hypnotic language pattern might actually help you indirectly do and achieve more positive results in whatever situation you have in mind.

Why Is This Hypnotic Language Pattern Important To Learn

It is important to learn this hypnotic language pattern because it will go a long way in improving your communication skills. This is because it gives you the effective persuasion skill to make even the most difficult person be receptive to what you are offering. Once you have known how to use this effectively, you will be able to apply them in your business, job or in relationships to achieve the results you want. It is a great way of helping you indirectly achieve the goals you have set for yourself.

What You Need To Know About This Hypnotic Language Pattern

When using the 'how would you feel_____' hypnotic language pattern, you are actually in a subtle way, appealing to the persons emotional side for an answer. By doing this, the person is already imagining themselves in that situation, and actually feel and see the benefit of it. This therefore makes the person more receptive to whatever suggestions you make to them, while they are in that emotional state. It therefore helps that person mentally and emotional agreeable to what you are trying to persuade them to believe and act on.

How To Use This Hypnotic Language Pattern To Effectively Win People Over To Your Persuasions

This can be used in many different situations. You first of all have be clear about what you want to achieve by persuading that person. The person has to be able to visualize whatever it is you are suggesting. You then appeal to their emotional side by asking the 'How would you feel_____?' question. If you are selling a car and you ask the client 'How would you feel if you could drive out with this car today'. Or 'How would you feel if you could go for your dream holiday in a month's time?' This question already puts the client in trance like state, because they are already imagining and visualizing themselves on holiday or driving that car. This therefore makes it easier for their unconscious mind to receive more information from you, In order to make a sale if you are a sales person.

How Else This Hypnotic Language Pattern Might Be Utilized Applicably In Other Useful Contexts

This pattern works the same way in whatever situation you have at hand be it in relationships or work related.

You simply ask the question and fill the gap with whatever you want that other person to feel. Once you have captured their emotional and mental side, they will be receptive to whatever other information you want to give them related to that question.

Final Purport

In this chapter I shared with you an astonishing hypnotic language pattern. I explained that it would help you achieve great results, in what you are trying to persuade someone about. I then shared with you 'why' you should commit to learning and using this hypnotic language pattern; emphasizing the effectiveness and how easy it is to use. Then I shared everything you needed to know about the hypnotic language pattern; namely: (a) how it works, (b) how to phrase it, and (c) and in what context to apply it. After explaining what you needed to know, I explained step-by-step 'how' you can use this hypnotic language pattern to achieve the results you desire. Explicitly, I told you that step one meant doing something to make the person visualize what you want to persuade them; that step two you should appeal to their emotional side and mental state by asking the 'How would you feel_____?' question, and step three you needed to make suggestions while they are in that emotional and mental state that will make that person make favorable decisions to you. Lastly, we explored some other ways this hypnotic language pattern might be useful. We took an interdisciplinary approach and decided that this hypnotic language pattern could be used in other contexts such as in trying to convince very difficult people. Used in these contexts the benefits one might realize could include: (a) achieving a sell, (b) getting someone to agree to your plan at work or home, and (c) or sealing a great deal.

Action Steps

There is a principle someone taught me once, which they labeled the 'Law of Action'. It basically claims, that you can learn anything, be the most brilliant mind, but if you don't take what you know and put it into action, it's worthless. I'm guilty of this, so let me be first to raise my own hand.

For years I learned information from reading books, attending seminars, being a student (I have multiple degrees), and still I remained broke, and sometimes penniless.

Then I read a book, and got inspired to take action, and start sharing all this knowledge with others. I took a job as a sales trainer, and taught others what I knew, and not surprisingly the company I contracted to prospered abundantly. Then I started my own company, and began experiencing huge results. Today, I have a new habit: I take what I learn and teach it to others, for profit of course, and I love it. Action is my best friend, and was the missing ingredient in my life. Since I learned this law, I have never looked back, and my life has become a lot more meaningful, and more richly rewarded.

All of this being said, I encourage you to do the following action steps; not because I want to waste your time, but because I want you to have the results you want. You should maximize the value of this book, and earn an exponential return on your investment, my opinion anyway!

I.   Take this pattern and use it on ten people, and observe critically the response you're given by the other person. Watch for their physiology, their voice tonality, and what they actually say. More important usually is not what is said, but 'how' it's said. The word 'how' relates to energy or quality. When someone's response is congruently aligned with their physiology they are usually telling the truth, and resistance is lessened or non-existent. If someone tells you what you want to hear, but their physiology isn't congruently aligned, assume the opposite.

II.   Write a journal entry on your experiences using this 'exact' hypnotic language pattern. Note whether or not you got closer to your desired outcome, or further away. Also note if the person complied and took action or not.

III. Make it a point to memorize this hypnotic language pattern now. The easiest way to do this is to use it on as many people as you can. Make it a part of your everyday language. Sooner or later you'll be using it unconsciously, and when you do you'll know that you're exactly where you need to be.

IV.   Teach this hypnotic language pattern to a friend or family member and explain what you've learned in this chapter to them. Perhaps this person will be someone whom you can feed patterns back and forth off of, to help you master these 25 hypnotic language patterns sooner.

V.   Get a 3x5 index card, and cut it in half vertically; namely, making two 'almost square' rectangles, and write this hypnotic language pattern on the front side. Below the pattern, make an abridged note to help you remember what contexts you should use the pattern in.

CHAPTER 20

Hypnotic Language Pattern Nineteen of Twenty-Five

HYPNOTIC LANGUAGE PATTERN

CAN YOU IMAGINE ___

In this chapter I'm going to be sharing with you an amazing hypnotic language pattern that is going to help you in increasing your ability to attract the attention of other people and influence them in a manner that yields positive dividends. First I'm going to share with you 'why' this is important, and talk about the important real time benefits of using this hypnotic language pattern. Then I'm going to be sharing with you 'what' you need to know about this particular 'hypnotic language pattern', specifically covering "can you imagine ____?" Next I'm going to literally explain to you 'how' you can use this hypnotic language pattern to achieve the desired result of influencing other people and get the desired results out of them. Finally, I'm going to explore with you some other ways this hypnotic language pattern might actually help you indirectly do things that are more persuasive in nature.

Why Is This Hypnotic Language Pattern Important To Learn

By learning the hypnotic pattern, "can you imagine it?" You would be able to get the needed confidence of saying things that can influence others. This pattern would help you to get the needed energy and confidence for taking on newer challenges and convert those challenges in to opportunities.

The reason for this is that asking questions takes the pressure off the speaker, and places it onto the person receiving the question. The subject, in order to know if they can 'imagine' something or not, must first imagine it. This means that regardless if they can or not, they have. You're in this way, indirectly influencing the hypnotic subject to think a certain thought. If you can get someone to think something you want them to think about, without raising suspicion in their conscious critical thinking mind, you stand a much better opportunity to receive the results and actions you desire from your subject.

What You Need To Know About This Hypnotic Language Pattern

This "Can you imagine _____?" would help you to visualize yourself in doing a particular thing that would bring you the required benefits in terms of determining whether you would be able to achieve your set objective. When you imagine yourself to be doing a particular activity, you would be able to instantly think through the benefits provided by acting in such a manner. When you ask this of your hypnotic subject, it causes them, likewise, to do the same and to consider things they might not have otherwise considered. Once they put some thought to something, they are more open-minded and likely to accept and comply with your persuasion arguments.

How To Use This Hypnotic Language Pattern To Effectively Win People Over To Your Persuasions

There are many situations in which this hypnotic pattern can be used. If you can imagine some of these different ways, before you have other people imaging them, then you can get a better idea of how other people will interpret and perceive them, when you do. This is one of the easiest ways to learn how you can apply this particular hypnotic language pattern appropriately to achieve the results you want. Take for instance someone who is stressed out because of relational issues with a partner. You can first imaging what this would be like. Take if you and your partner have been stressed out due to professional and domestic commitments and looking for a way out you can follow the following steps:

I.   You can imagine how it can be when you and your partner go on a relaxing vacation to some destination.

II.   When you imagine such a scenario, your mind would automatically get refreshed and start thinking in a positive manner

III. You can use the following "Can I?" pattern. "Can you imagine what it would be like if we went on a fun and relaxing Vacation together to Swiss Alps"

How Else This Hypnotic Language Pattern Might Be Utilized Applicably In Other Useful Contexts

Suppose you are working in a big team and you feel that you are often overlooked by your co-workers and also by your supervisors. In this situation, instead of feeling let down, you need to start imagining certain situations that might reverse the current judgment passed by your colleagues. You can make use of this "Can I" pattern to influence your co-workers—for example, "Can you imagine how your co-workers will respond when you are more persuasive and confident?"

Final Purport

In this chapter I shared with you an astonishing hypnotic language pattern. I explained that it would help you both in the personal front and also in the professional front. I then shared with you 'why' you should commit to learning and using this hypnotic pattern; emphasizing on sharpening your ability to influence others. Then I shared everything you needed to know about this hypnotic language pattern; namely: "can I pattern", (b) situations in which it can used, and (c) its benefits. After explaining what you needed to know, I explained step-by-step 'how' you can use this hypnotic language pattern to achieve the results you desire. Explicitly, I told you that step one meant doing imagining a situation that would prove a solution; that step two you should imagine to refresh your mind, and step three you needed to follow a particular "Can I pattern?". Lastly, we explored some other ways this hypnotic language pattern might be useful. We took an interdisciplinary approach and decided that this hypnotic language pattern could be used in other contexts such as positively influencing your colleagues. Used in these contexts the benefits one might realize could include: (a) the ability to influence others to your own advantage, (b) Delight your customers or audience and (c) help people to come out of a fixed mind set and realize their passion.

Action Steps

There is a principle someone taught me once, which they labeled the 'Law of Action'. It basically claims, that you can learn anything, be the most brilliant mind, but if you don't take what you know and put it into action, it's worthless. I'm guilty of this, so let me be first to raise my own hand.

For years I learned information from reading books, attending seminars, being a student (I have multiple degrees), and still I remained broke, and sometimes penniless.

Then I read a book, and got inspired to take action, and start sharing all this knowledge with others. I took a job as a sales trainer, and taught others what I knew, and not surprisingly the company I contracted to prospered abundantly. Then I started my own company, and began experiencing huge results. Today, I have a new habit: I take what I learn and teach it to others, for profit of course, and I love it. Action is my best friend, and was the missing ingredient in my life. Since I learned this law, I have never looked back, and my life has become a lot more meaningful, and more richly rewarded.

All of this being said, I encourage you to do the following action steps; not because I want to waste your time, but because I want you to have the results you want. You should maximize the value of this book, and earn an exponential return on your investment, my opinion anyway!

I.   Take this pattern and use it on ten people, and observe critically the response you're given by the other person. Watch for their physiology, their voice tonality, and what they actually say. More important usually is not what is said, but 'how' it's said. The word 'how' relates to energy or quality. When someone's response is congruently aligned with their physiology they are usually telling the truth, and resistance is lessened or non-existent. If someone tells you what you want to hear, but their physiology isn't congruently aligned, assume the opposite.

II.   Write a journal entry on your experiences using this 'exact' hypnotic language pattern. Note whether or not you got closer to your desired outcome, or further away. Also note if the person complied and took action or not.

III.   Make it a point to memorize this hypnotic language pattern now. The easiest way to do this is to use it on as many people as you can. Make it a part of your everyday language. Sooner or later you'll be using it unconsciously, and when you do you'll know that you're exactly where you need to be.

IV.   Teach this hypnotic language pattern to a friend or family member and explain what you've learned in this chapter to them. Perhaps

this person will be someone whom you can feed patterns back and forth off of, to help you master these 25 hypnotic language patterns sooner.

V.   Get a 3x5 index card, and cut it in half vertically; namely, making two 'almost square' rectangles, and write this hypnotic language pattern on the front side. Below the pattern, make an abridged note to help you remember what contexts you should use the pattern in.

Hypnotic Language Pattern Twenty of Twenty-Five

HYPNOTIC LANGUAGE PATTERN

THE AGREEMENT PATTERN [AND V. BUT]

In this chapter I'm going to be sharing with you an amazing hypnotic language pattern that is going to help you reduce resistance during a conversation. First I'm going to share with you 'why' it is important and discuss getting people to agree rather than resist you. Then I'm going to be sharing with you 'what' you need to know about this particular 'hypnotic language pattern', specifically covering its uses and benefits. Next I'm going to literally explain to you 'how' you can use this hypnotic language patter to achieve better sales results. Finally, I'm going to explore with you some other ways this hypnotic language pattern might actually help you indirectly influence people in your personal life.

Why Is This Hypnotic Language Pattern Important To Learn

We all use and are influenced by hypnotic language patterns regardless of whether we are aware of it or not. Understanding how we can use different words and speak in a manner which influences people's natural thought patterns to result in the desired behavior makes it simpler for us to convey the right messages when interacting with others. Using hypnotic language patterns can help you to persuade people's thoughts during negotiation processes, when expressing authority or criticism during presentations and sales meetings. In our economy, success is measured by our competence to communicate effectively. If you are a business owner, you'll want to influence clients in order to make more sales and build relationships as well as communicate effectively with staff. As an employee, you'll want to convey your value to potential employers and communicate well with colleagues. The effective use of hypnotic language patterns gives us confidence through the ability to exercise control over other people's thinking, imagination and their reaction towards us. This method is effective during any conversation on a professional or personal scale. In using the agreement pattern, we specifically influence people to agree rather than disagree with us. People are naturally drawn to people who they agree with so this will make it simpler to establish rapport and understanding with people.

What Do You Need To Know About This Hypnotic Language Pattern

Showing someone that you agree with them makes them more comfortable with you and at ease within the situation. Agreement is a resistance dropping cue which makes people feel at ease and comfortable with you, which can be used rather than risking unconsciously using resistance inducing phrases which push people away.

How To Use This Hypnotic Language Pattern To Effectively Win People Over To Your Persuasions

The agreement pattern is used by following these steps:

I.   Start your response with the words "I agree".

II. Use "and" as a conjunction in your statement rather than "but". The latter will make the listener aware that you are about to in some way invalidate the agreement you made in the first part of the sentence, whereas "and" tells them that you are simply adding to their statement or argument. An example illustrating this method is the following sentence; "I agree that the product has a high price tag and because of this you are guaranteed the best quality." That sentence will work better than; "I agree that the product has a high price tag but you are guaranteed the best quality."

III.   Speak with sincerity. This method is used to gain understanding and reduce resistance. A person will not drop their defense mechanisms if they believe you are insincere.

How Else This Hypnotic Language Pattern Might Be Utilized Applicably In Other Useful Contexts

This pattern is particularly useful in conflict situations. In a heated conversation, people are defensive and this will only be heightened by saying the wrong thing. Instead, when they feel like you agree with them, they will begin to drop their defenses and listen closer to what you have to say.

Final Purport

In this chapter I shared with you an astonishing hypnotic language pattern. I explained that it would help you achieve desired results during a conversation. I then shared with you 'why' you should commit to learning and using this hypnotic language pattern; emphasizing how it will help you put people at ease and make them more likely to agree with you. Then I shared everything you needed to know about the hypnotic language pattern; namely: how it is applied, in which context and to what extent. After explaining what you needed to know, I explained step-by-step 'how' you can use this hypnotic language pattern to achieve the results you desire. Explicitly, I told you that step one meant showing that you agree with the other person, that in step two you should use the word "and" instead of "but" and step three requires you to speak sincerely. Lastly, we explored some other ways this hypnotic language pattern might be useful. We took an interdisciplinary approach and decided that this hypnotic language pattern could be used in other contexts such as conflict situations and everyday conversations. Used in these contexts the benefits one might realize could include: getting positive responses from people and decreasing resistance and conflict.

Action Steps

There is a principle someone taught me once, which they labeled the 'Law of Action'. It basically claims, that you can learn anything, be the most brilliant mind, but if you don't take what you know and put it into action, it's worthless. I'm guilty of this, so let me be first to raise my own hand.

For years I learned information from reading books, attending seminars, being a student (I have multiple degrees), and still I remained broke, and sometimes penniless.

Then I read a book, and got inspired to take action, and start sharing all this knowledge with others. I took a job as a sales trainer, and taught others what I knew, and not surprisingly the company I contracted to prospered abundantly. Then I started my own company, and began experiencing huge results. Today, I have a new habit: I take what I learn and teach it to others, for profit of course, and I love it. Action is my best friend, and was the missing ingredient in my life. Since I learned this law, I have never looked back, and my life has become a lot more meaningful, and more richly rewarded.

All of this being said, I encourage you to do the following action steps; not because I want to waste your time, but because I want you to have the results you want. You should maximize the value of this book, and earn an exponential return on your investment, my opinion anyway!

I. Take this pattern and use it on ten people, and observe critically the response you're given by the other person. Watch for their physiology, their voice tonality, and what they actually say. More important usually is not what is said, but 'how' it's said. The word 'how' relates to energy or quality. When someone's response is congruently aligned with their physiology they are

usually telling the truth, and resistance is lessened or non-existent. If someone tells you what you want to hear, but their physiology isn't congruently aligned, assume the opposite.

II. Write a journal entry on your experiences using this 'exact' hypnotic language pattern. Note whether or not you got closer to your desired outcome, or further away. Also note if the person complied and took action or not.

III. Make it a point to memorize this hypnotic language pattern now. The easiest way to do this is to use it on as many people as you can. Make it a part of your everyday language. Sooner or later you'll be using it unconsciously, and when you do you'll know that you're exactly where you need to be.

IV. Teach this hypnotic language pattern to a friend or family member and explain what you've learned in this chapter to them. Perhaps this person will be someone whom you can feed patterns back and forth off of, to help you master these 25 hypnotic language patterns sooner.

V. Get a 3x5 index card, and cut it in half vertically; namely, making two 'almost square' rectangles, and write this hypnotic language

pattern on the front side. Below the pattern, make an abridged note to help you remember what contexts you should use the pattern in.

Hypnotic Language Pattern Twenty of Twenty-Five

HYPNOTIC LANGUAGE PATTERN

THE FACT THAT [FACT], MEANS ___

In this article I'm going to be sharing with you an amazing hypnotic language pattern that is going to help you make changes you may desire within your life. First I'm going to share with you 'why' this is important, and talk about how you can make changes in your life, using the knowledge that 'the fact that anything exists means there are near endless possibilities in accomplishing anything in life.

Then I'm going to be sharing with you 'what' you need to know about this particular 'hypnotic language pattern', specifically covering how 'The fact that [fact] means ___' applies to everyday life on all levels. Next I'm going to literally explain to you 'how' you can use this hypnotic language patter to achieve life changing benefits that will help you 'master' anything. Finally, I'm going to explore with you some other ways this hypnotic language pattern might actually help you indirectly do whatever one might desire in life.

Why Is This Hypnotic Language Pattern Important To Learn

The hypnotic language pattern 'The fact that [fact] means ___' presents an opportunity for people to learn how to 'master any complex skill,' as cited from the hypnotic pattern itself.

Taking that knowledge in mind, the main concept of the hypnotic pattern is 'The fact that [fact] means [blank]'. According to hypnotic logic, this refers to how people can state a fact: such as 'I exist') and say what the conversational hypnotist wants it to mean, (e.g., 'You can be sure I have your best interest at heart.'). Notice that what follows 'means' only has to be 'somewhat' plausible, to be believed.

The importance of this hypnotic language pattern lies in how people perceive themselves and their map of reality. If people acknowledge their existence for what it is, they may be able to accomplish anything, such as the mastering of complexities, as I'll cover in the next sections.

What You Need To Know About This Hypnotic Language Pattern

'The fact that [fact] means ___' presents an interesting opportunity for those well versed in hypnotic language (or not).

The main concept, as mentioned in the last section, states that we can state a fact, and then say what it means. Based on that concept, we can infer that stating a fact true to us, and then saying the meaning out loud, will help us realize the weight of that fact and its 'existence' to us and the world.

Saying things out loud, in a way, formalizes it and makes it 'real'. When we hear something stated to us aloud, we take what is said as fact. Speech, in general, holds a large influence and effect on people, something perhaps explaining why verbal hypnosis is effective.

Going by that, 'The fact that [fact] means ___' shows us potentially how acknowledging what's true about what we can accomplish (the facts) can help us 'hard wire' and imprint these ideas and thinking patterns into our subject's memory and, eventually, mold it to their cognitive functions.

How To Use This Hypnotic Language Pattern To Effectively Win People Over To Your Persuasions

Take a moment to state a fact about anything. Think about it, and then state what it means to you. Were you affected in some way? If so, do you think others would buy into the argument you posed?

What does it mean to you? If you state that: 'You write, and it means, you hold the potential to master any complex skill that draws upon all of our senses and cognitive functions. That example, demonstrates how 'The fact that [fact] means ___', shows how anything can be possible when you use this hypnotic language pattern.

If you desire to win over others to your persuasions, rely on social encouragement. Many people, even if not acknowledged, like looking up to someone who presents an opportunity to change them in a positive way. That's why leaders work well as leaders: because they know how to convince and guide others into achieving the idea that they will succeed.

I.   Step 1: State a fact, and then say what it means to them. What do they truly want?

II.   Step 2: Think of ways to apply that fact to what you can do for them. If they want to accomplish something, how can you persuade them to follow you into success?

III. Step 3: Present them with an opportunity and, together, work with them to achieve that.

How Else This Hypnotic Language Pattern Might Be Utilized Applicably In Other Useful Contexts

'The fact that [fact] means ____' works when applied to personal contexts, especially if using hypnotic language to change one's own life for the better.

As I mentioned in the previous section, stating something (out loud) makes it come to life. If you state it repeatedly, that exercise characterizes some of the self-hypnosis people use to correct problematic aspects of their life.

If something exists, factually, it presents an opportunity for your hypnotic subject to believe something else that is some generated idea has the potential to achieve a desired result for them. Many people, on a personal level, can infer that from 'The fact that [fact] means ____'.

Final Purport

In this article I shared with you an astonishing hypnotic language pattern. I explained that it would help you realize you can make changes in your life. I then shared with you 'why' you should commit to learning and using this hypnotic language pattern; emphasizing how 'formalizing' certain facts about ourselves will help us achieve our full potential; yet, the same rings true when we're helping others by using the hypnotic language pattern to get them to understand and see the potentiality of something possible and likely.

Then I shared everything you needed to know about the hypnotic language pattern; namely: (a) how it may persuade you, (b) its main concept, and (c) how it may help you persuade others. After explaining what you needed to know, I explained step-by-step 'how' you can use this hypnotic language pattern to achieve the results you desire with using it to affect change in others.

Explicitly, I told you that step one meant formalizing 'facts', step two you should think of how to apply this pattern to help others believe you easier and without you getting resistance from their conscious mind, and step three you needed to present them with an opportunity that was beneficial to them indirectly.

Lastly, we explored some other ways this hypnotic language pattern might be useful. We took an interdisciplinary approach and decided that this hypnotic language pattern could be used in other contexts such as self-hypnosis. Used in these contexts the benefits one might realize could include: (a) finding ways to grow confidence/self-esteem, (b) improving memory and cognitive functions, and (c) achieving personal success.

Action Steps

There is a principle someone taught me once, which they labeled the 'Law of Action'. It basically claims, that you can learn anything, be the most brilliant mind, but if you don't take what you know and put it into action, it's worthless. I'm guilty of this, so let me be first to raise my own hand.

For years I learned information from reading books, attending seminars, being a student (I have multiple degrees), and still I remained broke, and sometimes penniless.

Then I read a book, and got inspired to take action, and start sharing all this knowledge with others. I took a job as a sales trainer, and taught others what I knew, and not surprisingly the company I contracted to prospered abundantly. Then I started my own company, and began experiencing huge results. Today, I have a new habit: I take what I learn and teach it to others, for profit of course, and I love it. Action is my best friend, and was the missing ingredient in my life. Since I learned this law, I have never looked back, and my life has become a lot more meaningful, and more richly rewarded.

All of this being said, I encourage you to do the following action steps; not because I want to waste your time, but because I want you to have the results you want. You should maximize the value of this book, and earn an exponential return on your investment, my opinion anyway!

I. Take this pattern and use it on ten people, and observe critically the response you're given by the other person. Watch for their physiology, their voice tonality, and what they actually say. More important usually is not what is said, but 'how' it's said. The word 'how' relates to energy or quality. When someone's response is congruently aligned with their physiology they are

usually telling the truth, and resistance is lessened or non-existent. If someone tells you what you want to hear, but their physiology isn't congruently aligned, assume the opposite.

II.   Write a journal entry on your experiences using this 'exact' hypnotic language pattern. Note whether or not you got closer to your desired outcome, or further away. Also note if the person complied and took action or not.

III.   Make it a point to memorize this hypnotic language pattern now. The easiest way to do this is to use it on as many people as you can. Make it a part of your everyday language. Sooner or later you'll be using it unconsciously, and when you do you'll know that you're exactly where you need to be.

IV.   Teach this hypnotic language pattern to a friend or family member and explain what you've learned in this chapter to them. Perhaps this person will be someone whom you can feed patterns back and forth off of, to help you master these 25 hypnotic language patterns sooner.

V.   Get a 3x5 index card, and cut it in half vertically; namely, making two 'almost square' rectangles, and write this hypnotic language

pattern on the front side. Below the pattern, make an abridged note to help you remember what contexts you should use the pattern in.

CHAPTER 22

Hypnotic Language Pattern Twenty-One of Twenty-Five

HYPNOTIC LANGUAGE PATTERN

I'M CURIOUS TO KNOW IF ___

In this chapter I'm going to be sharing with you an amazing hypnotic language pattern that is going to help you make clients feel at ease, get answers easier and indirectly put the conversation totally in your control. First I'm going to share with you 'why' this is important, and talk about how to command the direction of a conversation without seeming intrusive or over-authoritative. Then I'm going to be sharing with you 'what' you need to know about this particular 'hypnotic language pattern', specifically covering how to successfully embed commands in one simple question. Next I'm going to literally explain to you 'how' you can use this hypnotic language patter to achieve a readiness from clients to follow your commands, turn any situation into a favorable one. Finally, I'm going to explore with you some other ways this hypnotic language pattern might actually help you indirectly influence people's decisions.

Why Is This Hypnotic Language Pattern Important To Learn

Indirect elicitation patterns are an absolutely crucial technique used to lead clients to exactly where you want them to be, without seeming pushy or intrusive (this applies to business as well). Commanding people to do this or that will put them on edge and make your job harder. As opposed to stating a command straight out, simply starting off with "I'm curious to know if..." will open the floodgates to greater rapport opportunities. Clients will be more honest, and more apt to open up to you because you are showing interest in them and their feelings. You don't simply want to know about them, you are curious about their life and feelings. It makes all the difference in the world.

What You Need To Know About This Hypnotic Language Pattern

This hypnotic language pattern is a command disguised as a simple inquiry into people's lives and thoughts. Imbedding a command will lead the client to be more open to your suggestions. It is therefore of the utmost importance to control your speech and the tone of your voice. Using a traditional 'command' will unmask your true intentions automatically and put people on edge. If, however, preceded by the docile-sounding "I'm curious to know if..." your command is no longer threatening. Rather, it is a great way to "soften" people up. A slight emphasis should be put on your command, using just a tiny difference in the tone of your voice.

How To Use Hypnotic Language Patterns To Effectively Win People Over To Your Persuasions

This hypnotic language pattern can be easily implemented in your practice, giving you the upper hand in any situation. It is a great way to win people over to your persuasions. On a conscious level, you are delving into one of mankind's favorite subjects-themselves. However, on an unconscious level, your 'curiosity' is the driving force leading them to follow your commands. Be sure to make it clear that you want to know about their feelings, their life. After your initial command, you can use their response to delve into the aspects of their life that you are interested in. Move the conversation slowly in your desired direction. While an overt show of your power and command will turn off many clients, this is the perfect way to smoothly move the conversation in the direction that you want it to move in. From there, gathering the information you seek is child's play.

How Else This Hypnotic Language Pattern Might Be Utilized Applicably In Other Useful Contexts

This language pattern is not only effective for hypnosis, but for life in general. In fact, embedding commands in everyday language can be applied in a variety of situations, especially the workplace. By discreetly masking your commands, co-workers will be more likely to accept your proposals. Your authority is not broadcasted or used as a threat to others, but rather, it is used to let you get what you want while appearing to be humble and interested in other's opinions. The great idea will be accredited to you, but, of course, it will also be a team effort. You are made to look like a born leader, the creator of amazing ideas and a person who can willingly get others to successfully complete a task.

Final Purport

In this chapter I shared with you an astonishing hypnotic language pattern. I explained that it would help you exert your authority in a covert manner. I then shared with you 'why' you should commit to learning and using this hypnotic language pattern; emphasizing the positive effects it will have in moving a situation in the direction you want to it go. Then I shared everything you needed to know about the hypnotic language pattern; namely controlling your speech and tone of voice. After explaining what you needed to know, I explained step-by-step 'how' you can use this hypnotic language pattern to achieve the results you desire. Explicitly, I told you that step one meant slyly embedding a command into a question you ask; that step two you should move the conversation slowly towards the subject you want to approach, and step three you needed to simply collect the information you seek. Lastly, we explored some other ways this hypnotic language pattern might be useful. We took an interdisciplinary approach and decided that this hypnotic language pattern could be used in other contexts such as the workplace. Used in these contexts the benefits one might realize could include: non-threatening authority, increased productivity, and all around respect.

Action Steps

There is a principle someone taught me once, which they labeled the 'Law of Action'. It basically claims, that you can learn anything, be the most brilliant mind, but if you don't take what you know and put it into action, it's worthless. I'm guilty of this, so let me be first to raise my own hand.

For years I learned information from reading books, attending seminars, being a student (I have multiple degrees), and still I remained broke, and sometimes penniless.

Then I read a book, and got inspired to take action, and start sharing all this knowledge with others. I took a job as a sales trainer, and taught others what I knew, and not surprisingly the company I contracted to prospered abundantly. Then I started my own company, and began experiencing huge results. Today, I have a new habit: I take what I learn and teach it to others, for profit of course, and I love it. Action is my best friend, and was the missing ingredient in my life. Since I learned this law, I have never looked back, and my life has become a lot more meaningful, and more richly rewarded.

All of this being said, I encourage you to do the following action steps; not because I want to waste your time, but because I want you to have the results you want. You should maximize the value of this book, and earn an exponential return on your investment, my opinion anyway!

I. Take this pattern and use it on ten people, and observe critically the response you're given by the other person. Watch for their physiology, their voice tonality, and what they actually say. More important usually is not what is said, but 'how' it's said. The word 'how' relates to energy or quality. When someone's response is congruently aligned with their physiology they are

usually telling the truth, and resistance is lessened or non-existent. If someone tells you what you want to hear, but their physiology isn't congruently aligned, assume the opposite.

II. Write a journal entry on your experiences using this 'exact' hypnotic language pattern. Note whether or not you got closer to your desired outcome, or further away. Also note if the person complied and took action or not.

III. Make it a point to memorize this hypnotic language pattern now. The easiest way to do this is to use it on as many people as you can. Make it a part of your everyday language. Sooner or later you'll be using it unconsciously, and when you do you'll know that you're exactly where you need to be.

IV. Teach this hypnotic language pattern to a friend or family member and explain what you've learned in this chapter to them. Perhaps this person will be someone whom you can feed patterns back and forth off of, to help you master these 25 hypnotic language patterns sooner.

V. Get a 3x5 index card, and cut it in half vertically; namely, making two 'almost square' rectangles, and write this hypnotic language

pattern on the front side. Below the pattern, make an abridged note to help you remember what contexts you should use the pattern in.

CHAPTER 23

Hypnotic Language Patterns Twenty-Two of Twenty-Five

HYPNOTIC LANGUAGE PATTERN

ONE OF THE THINGS YOU'RE GOING TO LOVE WITH THIS ___, IS ___.

In this chapter I'm going to be sharing with you an amazing hypnotic language pattern that is going to help you illicit positive thought processes from clients and preprogram them to accepting your proposal. First I'm going to share with you 'why' this is important, and talk about how to easily put your client in a positive mindset. Then I'm going to be sharing with you 'what' you need to know about this particular 'hypnotic language pattern', specifically covering one key element to avoid at all costs. Next I'm going to literally explain to you 'how' you can use this hypnotic language patter to achieve a close, friendly rapport with your client, put them in a positive mood and gently condition them to accept your proposals. Finally, I'm going to explore with you some other ways this hypnotic language pattern might actually help you indirectly improve how people view you and control their responses to you.

Why Is This Hypnotic Language Pattern Important To Learn

When working, you have a specific goal in mind. Whether it is to persuade clients to try a new method of something, or simply to impart your enthusiasm about a subject, you must lead the client exactly where you want to them to go. To achieve this goal, presupposition is a vital tool for a few reasons. First and foremost, you share your enthusiasm. "One of the things you're going to love with this _____ is..." You already love it, you are positive, and you are enthusiastic. These sentiments are passed on to the client, getting them interested in a subject that has you so excited. By using this technique, you have already decided the client's reaction will be positive. Finally, by using this phrase you subconsciously alert the client that there are, in reality, multiple aspects of your product to love.

What Do You Need To Know About This Hypnotic Language Pattern

This technique seems easy to implement, and it is. However, there are a few important points to keep in mind. From the beginning, the client is gently put in a positive mindset. This works in your favor. The client will undoubtedly feel excited about the product or service you offer and they trust you to deliver. It is here where a potential problem could arise. If your product or service does not meet the expectations you create in your clients, this technique can backfire. Do not exaggerate or promote aspects of your product or service that may not be 100% perfect yet. Focus on the strong selling points, things that you offer that no one else can. It is always easier to keep the customer in a positive mindset than have to try to re-convince them of your product's value.

How To Use This Hypnotic Language Pattern To Effectively Win People Over To Your Persuasions

One of the reasons why this technique is so successful is your interaction with the client and your interest in them. You are not mindlessly spouting off facts and figures. Actually, this persuasive technique makes it seem like you already know your client (even if you don't). They are not anonymous faces in a crowd- they are people who you have thought about enough to know why they will love what you are offering. You know what they like and what specific qualities they will appreciate. The client should feel as if you are interested in their satisfaction only, thanks to your superior product. When your product meets or, hopefully, exceeds their expectations, your position as a person who delivers on what they promise is sealed.

Regarding how specifically this pattern can be used you can:

I.   Watch for signs of excitement or talk of ownership (e.g., "I could…" or "If I take it…" or "Let's say I do get it…") and wait your turn to speak/answer your potential customer.

II.   Deliver this language pattern; filling in the blanks with whatever it is you're potential customer hopes to 'have/own' regarding a specific feature, advantage, or benefit.

III.   Recap immediately on the specific feature, explain how it creates the specific logical advantage that your prospect wants, and then explain how fulfilling that problem/need/greed, will cause an emotional benefit to happen about as well. This compounds the effect of the "One of the things you're going to love with this ___ is …" pattern.

How Else This Hypnotic Language Pattern Might Be Utilized Applicably In Other Useful Contexts

Presupposition is such a useful hypnotic language pattern because it can be applied to so many different situations every day. It not only changes how you are perceived in a positive way, but it also helps you to condition people. Whether in the workplace, social situations or at home, it is much more pleasant to interact with a positive person. You "love" what you have to offer and thus, are viewed in an optimistic manner. By noting the most outstanding aspects of your product or idea, you detract from parts that have not reached completion or perfection yet. In the workplace, this can be a vital technique to stay on top of your game.

Final Purport

In this chapter I shared with you an astonishing hypnotic language pattern. I explained that it would help you show your product, service or idea in a positive light and condition your client to accepting what you have to offer. I then shared with you 'why' you should commit to learning and using this hypnotic language pattern; emphasizing what an easy, but effective, technique it is. Then I shared everything you needed to know about the hypnotic language pattern; namely: how to start off on the right foot, how to endear yourself to your clients, and how to leave them happy. After explaining what you needed to know, I explained step-by-step 'how' you can use this hypnotic language pattern to achieve the results you desire. Explicitly, I told you that step one meant showing your enthusiasm; that step two you should foster this same sentiment in your clients, and step three you needed to deliver on your promises. Lastly, we explored some other ways this hypnotic language pattern might be useful. We took an interdisciplinary approach and decided that this hypnotic language pattern could be used in other contexts such as work or social situations. Used in these contexts the benefits one might realize could include: extra time to finalize unfinished details of a project, others viewing you in a positive light and having the advantage of being able to convince your clients of your product's superiority.

Action Steps

There is a principle someone taught me once, which they labeled the 'Law of Action'. It basically claims, that you can learn anything, be the most brilliant mind, but if you don't take what you know and put it into action, it's worthless. I'm guilty of this, so let me be first to raise my own hand.

For years I learned information from reading books, attending seminars, being a student (I have multiple degrees), and still I remained broke, and sometimes penniless.

Then I read a book, and got inspired to take action, and start sharing all this knowledge with others. I took a job as a sales trainer, and taught others what I knew, and not

surprisingly the company I contracted to prospered abundantly. Then I started my own company, and began experiencing huge results. Today, I have a new habit: I take what I learn and teach it to others, for profit of course, and I love it. Action is my best friend, and was the missing ingredient in my life. Since I learned this law, I have never looked back, and my life has become a lot more meaningful, and more richly rewarded.

All of this being said, I encourage you to do the following action steps; not because I want to waste your time, but because I want you to have the results you want. You should maximize the value of this book, and earn an exponential return on your investment, my opinion anyway!

I.   Take this pattern and use it on ten people, and observe critically the response you're given by the other person. Watch for their physiology, their voice tonality, and what they actually say. More important usually is not what is said, but 'how' it's said. The word 'how' relates to energy or quality. When someone's response is congruently aligned with their physiology they are usually telling the truth, and resistance is lessened or non-existent. If someone tells you what you want to hear, but their physiology isn't congruently aligned, assume the opposite.

II.   Write a journal entry on your experiences using this 'exact' hypnotic language pattern. Note whether or not you got closer to your desired

outcome, or further away. Also note if the person complied and took action or not.

III.   Make it a point to memorize this hypnotic language pattern now. The easiest way to do this is to use it on as many people as you can. Make it a part of your everyday language. Sooner or later you'll be using it unconsciously, and when you do you'll know that you're exactly where you need to be.

IV.   Teach this hypnotic language pattern to a friend or family member and explain what you've learned in this chapter to them. Perhaps this person will be someone whom you can feed patterns back and forth off of, to help you master these 25 hypnotic language patterns sooner.

V.   Get a 3x5 index card, and cut it in half vertically; namely, making two 'almost square' rectangles, and write this hypnotic language pattern on the front side. Below the pattern, make an abridged note to help you remember what contexts you should use the pattern in.

CHAPTER 24

Hypnotic Language Pattern Twenty-Three of Twenty-Five

HYPNOTIC LANGUAGE PATTERN

PACING AND LEADING PATTERN

In this chapter am going to share with you an amazing hypnotic language pattern that is going to help you learn the benefits of pacing and leading. These skills are essential in linguistic brain programing and are both effective when dealing with large audiences or individuals. First, am going to share with you "why" this is important and talk about how to pace and lead while ensuring your audience gets your message effectively. Then am going to share with you "what" you need me know about this particular hypnotic language pattern; specifically covering persuasive skills to win the hearts if your audience. Next I am going to literally explain to you "how" you can use the hypnotic language pattern better to achieve your persuasive goals through speech. Finally, am going to explore with you some other ways this hypnotic language pattern might actually help you indirectly to use factual and verifiable facts of pacing and leading for your subjects to agree with you.

Why Is This Hypnotic Language Pattern Important To Learn

Learning pacing and leading is an import investment since this enables you influence others through self-immersion. Leading and pacing as a hypnotic language pattern is not coercive thus giving your subjects a leeway to agree or disagree. This hypnotic language pattern "hypnotizes" your subjects once applied correctly and will always take your speech positively. The techniques used in this language pattern enables your listeners immerse their minds in the subject making them agree in a shorter period of time which is every speaker's goal or intend.

What You Need To Know About This Hypnotic Language Pattern

There some simple facts that you need to know about pacing and leading as a form of hypnotic language pattern;

it captures other people's imaginations and creates a chain of agreements. When correctly used pacing and leading hypnotic language pattern influences without cohesion but subconsciously help your subject in to a trace which enables them agree to your ideas.

How To Use This Hypnotic Language Pattern To Effectively Win People Over To Your Persuasions

One of the easiest way that you can effectively use pacing and leading hypnotic language pattern is by employing a series of simple questions which come with affirmative or yes answers. To make it easier, conditional questions which are somehow leading gives your subjects only one option; a yes answer. Using a speech or statements which have verifiable facts makes pacing and leading easy to win-over your audience since it imparts in them trust and confidence thus believing in you. Last but not least is the use of the correct verbal and nonverbal antidotes while keeping your audience engaged. Once you use this technique, you draw their attention thus convincing their mind-set to agree with what you are communicating.

How Else This Hypnotic Language Pattern Might Be Utilized Applicably In Other Useful Contexts

Leading and pacing hypnotic language pattern uses a technique that helps you in conditioning your subjects to agree to your speech. When used effectively, many sales people as well as decision makers have been able to influence their subjects positively. Through the use of pacing and leading hypnotic language pattern on the other hand, it becomes easy to convert adorers to users of your product or service. Through neurological conditioning, you can use this language pattern to convince your audience to adore what they have abhorred in the past. This hypnotic language pattern is essential in easing objections due to its persuasive nature; however how the subject rejects your first try, they eventually agree to your opinion.

Final Purport

In this chapter, I shared with you an astonishing hypnotic language pattern. I explained it would help you win others to your favor, break rejection barriers and "hypnotize" your audience and make them follow your line of thinking without any coercion. I then shared with you 'why' you should commit to learning and using this hypnotic language pattern emphasizing the it easily appeals to your audience, leads to a chain of agreements and enables subjects make quick decisions following your speech content. Then I shared everything you needed to know about the hypnotic language pattern; namely the use of leading questions, has verifiable facts and helps in tuning your subject's minds. After explaining what you needed to know, I explained step by step 'how' you can use the hypnotic language pattern to achieve the results you desire. Explicitly, I told you that step one meant doing use simple leading questions that step two you should be factual and step three you needed to select the appropriate nonverbal language. Lastly, we explored some other ways this hypnotic language pattern might be useful. We took an interdisciplinary approach and decided that this hypnotic language pattern could be used in other contexts such as sales pitching and influencing decision makers. Used in these contexts the benefits one might realize include and are not limited to making your audience agree with you, take less time to make decisions, and win others through persuasion.

Action Steps

There is a principle someone taught me once, which they labeled the 'Law of Action'. It basically claims, that you can learn anything, be the most brilliant mind, but if you don't take what you know and put it into action, it's worthless. I'm guilty of this, so let me be first to raise my own hand.

For years I learned information from reading books, attending seminars, being a student (I have multiple degrees), and still I remained broke, and sometimes penniless.

Then I read a book, and got inspired to take action, and start sharing all this knowledge with others. I took a job as a sales trainer, and taught others what I knew, and not surprisingly the company I contracted to prospered abundantly. Then I started my own company, and began experiencing huge results. Today, I have a new habit: I take what I learn and teach it to others, for profit of course, and I love it. Action is my best friend, and was the missing ingredient in my life. Since I learned this law, I have never looked back, and my life has become a lot more meaningful, and more richly rewarded.

All of this being said, I encourage you to do the following action steps; not because I want to waste your time, but because I want you to have the results you want. You should maximize the value of this book, and earn an exponential return on your investment, my opinion anyway!

I.   Take this pattern and use it on ten people, and observe critically the response you're given by the other person. Watch for their physiology, their voice tonality, and what they actually say. More important usually is not what is said, but 'how' it's said. The word 'how' relates to energy or quality. When someone's response is congruently aligned with their physiology they are usually telling the truth, and resistance is lessened or non-existent. If someone tells you what you want to hear, but their physiology isn't congruently aligned, assume the opposite.

II.   Write a journal entry on your experiences using this 'exact' hypnotic language pattern. Note whether or not you got closer to your desired outcome, or further away. Also note if the person complied and took action or not.

III.   Make it a point to memorize this hypnotic language pattern now. The easiest way to do this
is to use it on as many people as you can. Make
it a part of your everyday language. Sooner or
later you'll be using it unconsciously, and when
you do you'll know that you're exactly where
you need to be.

IV.   Teach this hypnotic language pattern to a
friend or family member and explain what
you've learned in this chapter to them. Perhaps
this person will be someone whom you can
feed patterns back and forth off of, to help you
master these 25 hypnotic language patterns
sooner.

V.   Get a 3x5 index card, and cut it in half vertically; namely, making two 'almost square' rectangles, and write this hypnotic language
pattern on the front side. Below the pattern,
make an abridged note to help you remember
what contexts you should use the pattern in.

CHAPTER 25

Hypnotic Language Pattern Twenty-Four of Twenty-Five

HYPNOTIC LANGUAGE PATTERN

[NAME] SAID "_____".

In this chapter I'm going to be sharing with you an amazing hypnotic language pattern that is going to help yield both parties positive results and give a solution to problems. First I'm going to share with you 'why' this pattern is important, and talk about importance and benefits of using this language pattern. Then I'm going to be sharing with you 'what' you need to know about this particular 'hypnotic language pattern', specifically covering the pattern: [Name] said "_____". Next I'm going to literally explain to you 'how' you can use this hypnotic language pattern to make people more comfortable and more relaxed around you by making their mind rewind to the "good times" from the past that represent nostalgic "good memories". Finally, I'm going to explore with you some other ways this hypnotic language pattern might actually help you indirectly do things that are more persuasive in nature with you hypnotic subject.

Why Is This Hypnotic Language Pattern Important To Learn

This hypnotic pattern [Name] said "_____" is important to learn because this pattern will help you determine what people want to achieve or avoid. It also helps take the pressure off of you the conversational hypnotist, because it's not you saying something, but rather someone else making the declaration. By using [Name] said "_____"hypnotic pattern you can communicate to your subject's hypnotic mind and lead them into a discussion in a way you want to.

The key thing to remember about this pattern is we use it all the time. We say statements like: "Well, John and Jane said, if we join their network marketing company, we'll be earning five thousand dollars per month, after only six months." This hypnotic language pattern is used often as a 'testimonial'. People are more apt to believe other people, over you. If you use this pattern to influence others, you're taking the pressure off the sale of your ideal, because it's not you making the claim, but someone else—someone not there.

What You Need To Know About This Hypnotic Language Pattern

Hypnotic pattern [Name] said "_____" works on the same concept as a statement without any critical judgment. The line following [name] said "_____" in meant to be implicitly true without any questions. Acceptance is the key to relaxation and [Name] said "_____" does just that. It also helps you to know what is going on inside someone's hypnotic mind, since when you deliver this pattern you'll instantly be able to tell looking at the subject's non-verbal communication and body language what's going on inside their mind. When you use this pattern the pressure is off of you being judged, and the subject feels more able to express their opinions, because they're not feeling pressured by you, but rather someone not there.

I love this pattern, because we're all influenced by people we're around, and this pattern allows you to influence and bring people over to your persuasions by having them be influenced and persuaded by total imaginary people who aren't there. There's power in numbers, and you can have as many people backing you as possible, even though they aren't there. It has in incredible impact on the hypnotic subject. They start to release and let go of their resistance, as you present the argument from the point of view of other people.

How To Use This Hypnotic Language Pattern To Effectively Win People Over To Your Persuasions

There are many situations in which this hypnotic language pattern can be used. For example, let's consider a situation when your friend or spouse did something to you, which you didn't like and are became pretty stressed about: Go back and think about their defensive argument when you communicated your feeling to them. Chances are they brought in other people to support their case, and chances are those people weren't even present for you to question. Notice how effective this technique was in their defense. Well, you can do the same thing in the future, and even in situations when your spouse or friend is bringing in other people to help defend their position, you can do the same as well, to support your offensive argument.

You can use [Name] said "_____" to take your state of mind from one of being stressed to relaxation by following the given steps:

1) Asking about anything pleasant that the spouse or friend said in the near past or before this thing happened.

2) Knowing the bonding between you two at that time you can realize that things between you two were good. And can be good in the future.

3) Going to old memories will help you continue thinking positively about him/her and make you realize he/she may have done it by mistake, or that all this can be a big nothing.

4) Positive thinking will help you relax as good thoughts are always triggered by good feelings and these good feelings will help you relax.

5) In a relaxed state you can decide more clearly how to present your argument in an 'indirect' way to ensure the situation doesn't happen again.

How Else This Hypnotic Language Pattern Might Be Utilized Applicably In Other Useful Contexts

Suppose you have done something, which you shouldn't have done, and you carry the guilt of doing or saying that thing. Realizing that other people have done the same thing, and that you're no better or worse a person than them can be useful in the forgiveness process.

[Name] said "_____" hypnotic pattern can help you influence other people as well, simply by pointing out the fact that other people are in agreement with your thinking, and not in agreement with your subject's current thinking. This can be helpful in sales and negotiation circumstances—for example, you can tell someone why they should behave, believe, and think a certain way, but chances are they'll not take you quite as seriously, than say if you bring other people into the argument who would never act that way, or believe those beliefs, or think those types of thoughts. You can say, Jane, said, "People who believe in false gods are doomed to go to hell." Jack said, the same thing. Also, John. You know how smart 'John' is, and how wise and kind 'Jane' is, so don't you think you can trust them and that what they tell you is true? I'm just saying... And so you see how this pattern can be applied to persuading someone into a particular religion, but realize it can be applied to just about any context. The key is to use trustworthy and notable people when you use this pattern, as the people who aren't there, but said "___".

Final Purport

In this chapter I shared with you an astonishing hypnotic language pattern. I explained that it would help you generate positive thoughts. I then shared with you 'why' you should commit to learning and using this hypnotic language pattern; emphasizing on improving your abilities to influence others. Then I shared everything you needed to know about this hypnotic language pattern; namely: (a) [name] said "_____" pattern, (b) how to use this pattern, and (c) the benefits of using this pattern. After explaining what you needed to know, I explained step-by-step 'how' you can use this hypnotic language pattern to trigger good feelings in your hypnotic subject, but also yourself.

Explicitly, I told you that step one meant having them remember some good old things that had happened in their past (or you remembering some good event from your past); that step two meant having them not cloud their judgment by present situational thinking, and; step three you needed to think whether the thing happened was intentional or simply by mistake.

Lastly, we explored some other ways this hypnotic language pattern might be useful: We took an interdisciplinary approach and decided that this hypnotic language pattern could be used in other contexts such as getting rid of guilt. Used in these contexts the benefits one might realize could include: (a) the ability to influence others, (b) attract a larger audience of devout followers, and (c) reach a rapport level that relaxes you and your hypnotic subject.

Action Steps

There is a principle someone taught me once, which they labeled the 'Law of Action'. It basically claims, that you can learn anything, be the most brilliant mind, but if you don't take what you know and put it into action, it's worthless. I'm guilty of this, so let me be first to raise my own hand.

For years I learned information from reading books, attending seminars, being a student (I have multiple degrees), and still I remained broke, and sometimes penniless.

Then I read a book, and got inspired to take action, and start sharing all this knowledge with others. I took a job as a sales trainer, and taught others what I knew, and not surprisingly the company I contracted to prospered abundantly. Then I started my own company, and began experiencing huge results. Today, I have a new habit: I take what I learn and teach it to others, for profit of course, and I love it. Action is my best friend, and was the missing ingredient in my life. Since I learned this law, I have never looked back, and my life has become a lot more meaningful, and more richly rewarded.

All of this being said, I encourage you to do the following action steps; not because I want to waste your time, but because I want you to have the results you want. You should maximize the value of this book, and earn an exponential return on your investment, my opinion anyway!

I. Take this pattern and use it on ten people, and observe critically the response you're given by the other person. Watch for their physiology, their voice tonality, and what they actually say. More important usually is not what is said, but 'how' it's said. The word 'how' relates to energy or quality. When someone's response is congruently aligned with their physiology they are usually telling the truth, and resistance is lessened or non-existent. If someone tells you what you want to hear, but their physiology isn't congruently aligned, assume the opposite.

II. Write a journal entry on your experiences using this 'exact' hypnotic language pattern. Note whether or not you got closer to your desired outcome, or further away. Also note if the person complied and took action or not.

III. Make it a point to memorize this hypnotic language pattern now. The easiest way to do this is to use it on as many people as you can. Make it a part of your everyday language. Sooner or later you'll be using it unconsciously, and when you do you'll know that you're exactly where you need to be.

IV.   Teach this hypnotic language pattern to a friend or family member and explain what you've learned in this chapter to them. Perhaps this person will be someone whom you can feed patterns back and forth off of, to help you master these 25 hypnotic language patterns sooner.

V.   Get a 3x5 index card, and cut it in half vertically; namely, making two 'almost square' rectangles, and write this hypnotic language pattern on the front side. Below the pattern, make an abridged note to help you remember what contexts you should use the pattern in.

CHAPTER 26

Hypnotic Language Pattern Twenty-Five of Twenty-Five

HYPNOTIC LANGUAGE PATTERN

WOULD YOU BE SURPRISED IF, ___

YOU PROBABLY ALREADY KNOW, ___

IF YOU COULD ___, WOULD YOU ___

In this chapter I'm going to be sharing with you an amazing hypnotic language pattern, and a couple others as well, that are going to help you overcome resistance, and focus your subject's awareness. First I'm going to share with you 'why' this is important, and talk about dealing with difficult people. Then I'm going to be sharing with you 'what' you need to know about this particular 'hypnotic language pattern', specifically covering the use of questions. Next I'm going to literally explain to you 'how' you can use this hypnotic language pattern to achieve the end results that you want. Finally, I'm going to explore with you some other ways this hypnotic language pattern might actually help you indirectly avoid potential objections.

Why Is This Hypnotic Language Pattern Important To Learn

We have to deal with difficult people in all aspects of our life and these techniques can be adapted to fit into any given situation. When you are wanting to have someone come around to your way of thinking or to agree to a proposal of yours, it would be good to know that you can do this without them suspecting they are being manipulated. By implanting thoughts into their heads you will slowly break down their resistance and be well on the way to getting the outcome that you wanted. This helps to overcome any objections that they may be thinking as you are taking down the path that you have chosen and getting them to more or less agree with what you are saying.

What You Need To Know About This Hypnotic Language Pattern

For starters, you need to know this hypnotic language pattern, because it puts you in control of the situation by asking questions that your hypnotic subject can only answer in the positive. If you say to them "Would you be surprised if, ___" people generally say no or yes. You then know what to say next depending on the context of the conversation. When you say to someone "You probably already know, ___" They are reluctant to say that they do not know and you can then carry on with your next point. By saying to someone "If you could choose to do either A or B which would you choose." Again you are limiting the scope for any resistance and bringing them round to the path that you are wanting.

How To Use This Hypnotic Language Pattern To Effectively Win People Over To Your Persuasions

By asking questions that you know they can only answer the way you want you are in total control of the conversation. By using the phrase "Imagine if, ___" you are planting the seeds in their mind of what you want them to think. You can gradually get them to see and agree that what you are saying makes sense. If they are trying to imagine the scenario that you have outlined they will not be thinking of ways to disagree with you and will not therefore have any objections when you move on.

How Else This Hypnotic Language Pattern Might Be Utilized Applicably In Other Useful Contexts

When dealing with children you will find that they can be the most difficult and unreasonable people you can meet. Children are affected emotionally easily, as it is their internal teaching mechanism that tells them when something is 'right' or 'wrong' and works to gage their behavior. Children are also some of the best, perhaps the best, persuaders in the world, because they can affect us at a deep emotional level when they ask for something. They also never give up when asking for something they want. Their pleas can make it difficult for us adults to say 'no!' to. By asking the right questions and limiting the scope for any answers that you don't want to hear, you can bring them round to see your point of view and get them to realize that their behavior is irrational and that your way is right. Other family members can be subjected to this method to avoid any heated arguments and quickly diffuse any situations that may escalate.

Final Purport

In this chapter I shared with you an astonishing hypnotic language pattern. I explained that it would help you overcome resistance and be more persuasive. I then shared with you 'why' you should commit to learning and using this hypnotic language pattern; emphasizing getting the outcome that you want. Then I shared everything you needed to know about the hypnotic language pattern; namely: (a) questioning, (b) using stock phrases, and (c) achieving your goal. After explaining what you needed to know, I explained step-by-step 'how' you can use this hypnotic language pattern to achieve the results you desire. Explicitly, I told you that step one meant doing questioning; that step two you should take control, and step three you needed to be positive. Lastly, we explored some other ways this hypnotic language pattern might be useful. We took an interdisciplinary approach and decided that this hypnotic language pattern could be used in other contexts such as dealing with children. Used in these contexts the benefits one might realize could include: (a) improved behavior, (b) dealing with awkward situations, and (c) overcoming resistance.

Action Steps

There is a principle someone taught me once, which they labeled the 'Law of Action'. It basically claims, that you can learn anything, be the most brilliant mind, but if you don't take what you know and put it into action, it's worthless. I'm guilty of this, so let me be first to raise my own hand.

For years I learned information from reading books, attending seminars, being a student (I have multiple degrees), and still I remained broke, and sometimes penniless.

Then I read a book, and got inspired to take action, and start sharing all this knowledge with others. I took a job as a sales trainer, and taught others what I knew, and not surprisingly the company I contracted to prospered abundantly. Then I started my own company, and began experiencing huge results. Today, I have a new habit: I take what I learn and teach it to others, for profit of course, and I love it. Action is my best friend, and was the missing ingredient in my life. Since I learned this law, I have never looked back, and my life has become a lot more meaningful, and more richly rewarded.

All of this being said, I encourage you to do the following action steps; not because I want to waste your time, but because I want you to have the results you want. You should maximize the value of this book, and earn an exponential return on your investment, my opinion anyway!

I.   Take this pattern and use it on ten people, and observe critically the response you're given by the other person. Watch for their physiology, their voice tonality, and what they actually say. More important usually is not what is said, but 'how' it's said. The word 'how' relates to energy or quality. When someone's response is congruently aligned with their physiology they are usually telling the truth, and resistance is lessened or non-existent. If someone tells you what you want to hear, but their physiology isn't congruently aligned, assume the opposite.

II.   Write a journal entry on your experiences using this 'exact' hypnotic language pattern. Note whether or not you got closer to your desired outcome, or further away. Also note if the person complied and took action or not.

III.   Make it a point to memorize this hypnotic language pattern now. The easiest way to do this is to use it on as many people as you can. Make it a part of your everyday language. Sooner or later you'll be using it unconsciously, and when you do you'll know that you're exactly where you need to be.

IV.   Teach this hypnotic language pattern to a friend or family member and explain what you've learned in this chapter to them. Perhaps this person will be someone whom you can feed patterns back and forth off of, to help you master these 25 hypnotic language patterns sooner.

V.   Get a 3x5 index card, and cut it in half vertically; namely, making two 'almost square' rectangles, and write this hypnotic language pattern on the front side. Below the pattern, make an abridged note to help you remember what contexts you should use the pattern in.

CHAPTER 27

A Final Recap on Hypnotic Language Patterns; And an After Thought

We've made it to the end, nearly. I hope you've gotten a ton of value from this book already. There's a lot to say about hypnotic language patterns. There are many, many, to learn. You can learn many of them straight from off my website FREE without any commitment to buy another product from me. I think, however, you'll find that I have a lot to offer you, and hopefully you'll take the time to invest in learning more about hypnotic language, and other communication skillsets that I teach on the blog, and through my product offerings.

I had you do action steps for each of the chapters. You probably noticed straight away that they were all the same, for every chapter, and I didn't do that just to fill up space in this book. I did it with a clear purpose in mind: If you

238 • BRYAN WESTRA

took the time to do all the actions I recommended, you have by now a small deck of flashcards, and some understanding of how the language patterns work, and how you'll want to use them for your own influence and persuasion purposes. Assuming you did all the actions you also have most if not all of the language patterns memorized, and have been practicing them with everybody you encounter and engage in a conversation (or with people who perhaps have engaged you in conversation).

It is important, now, that we recap some on the purpose of hypnotic language. I started you off in general terms, explaining the benefits, and how you might yourself benefit from using the hypnotic language patterns; then we delved into each individual language pattern itself, learning why each one was important, what you needed to know about each one, how to actually apply the language pattern to your everyday circumstances, and we even stepped outside the box (metaphorically speaking) to consider other ways each language pattern could be utilized outside the contexts we discussed in each chapter; and, now, it's time to chunk back up to the general and round all of these language patterns off, thematically, so you start to see how they work collectively.

I've enjoyed teaching you these language patterns. I hope you've taken the time to learn them, committed them to memory, and practiced them often as you went through each chapter of this book, learning new patterns. If you have, you know a lot more than most seasoned hypnotists and sales professionals do, when it comes to hypnotic language mastery. This means, you'll be able to (without using a script) communicate hypnotically and deepen your subject's hypnotic trances, beyond what most other hypnotists and persuasion artists might be able to.

Finally, I'm going to be sharing with you more about hypnotic language patters that will help you further your working-knowledge of conversational hypnosis without having to spend hours of detailed research. First I'm going to share with you 'why' this is important, and talk about why hypnotic language patterns are important. Then I'm going to be sharing with you 'what' you need to know about 'hypnotic language patterns'; specifically covering how to solidify specific techniques to be used in casual and business conversations. Next I'm going to literally explain to you 'how' you can use hypnotic language patterns to achieve and understand the true power of influence in conversations. Finally, I'm going to explore with you some other ways hypnotic language patterns might actually help you indirectly do and say things to truly navigate conversations toward your desired result and outcomes.

Why Are Hypnotic Language Patterns Important to Learn

Conversational hypnosis language patterns draw upon your own desires and objectives while introducing these desires in a powerful way to your subjects, i.e. the people you will be influencing and persuading. Throughout the various processes found in these patterns, you learned how to influence choices and instill distinct objectives within your listeners psyche. Through a progression combining knowledge and practical uses, learning these language patterns effectively altered your own interpersonal communication skills.

What You Need to Know About This Hypnotic Language Pattern

First and foremost, you must understand navigating the free will of listeners is not easily accomplished and you must be willing to accept outcomes that differ from your original intention. Conversations are fluid, and though predictable (as most behavior is) it still requires you to accept that sometimes even the best efforts don't turn-up the most desired outcomes. When situations like these occur remember that there's always another day, and that influencing people has to happen when it's supposed to happen. There's a natural progression, and not everybody is as easily influenced or persuaded as the great majority of people are. However, everyone can and is influenced and persuaded by other people. That being said, these particular hypnotic language patterns focus on supporting freely chosen choices by offering solid facts followed by suggestions. They also consist of awareness predicates that can be used to direct focus and attention to where you want and need for it to go, to better likely achieve your desired end result. To excel, you must fully learn individual techniques such as utilizing the power of suggestion words and techniques (because, can, etc. –and also report information and outline mental processes to create a greater

likelihood that your subject will comply with your suggestions). The true effects of these language patterns rest in
the truth; that is—a person may not know they are being
hypnotized, because it's only through communicating
with the hypnotic mind that true alterations to choices
and decisions are made.

How To Use This Hypnotic Language Pattern Effectively To Win People Over To Your Persuasions

Effectively winning over listeners by having them be
influenced through your words is no easy task; however,
the challenge is simplified when you understand how to
utilize subconscious language patterns to alter a subject's
choices. To effectively use these techniques, understand
that all other techniques are built upon the foundational
truth that listeners are unaware of your influence. Speak
with full confidence and conviction. These hypnotic language pattern techniques will fall flat if you do not operate
every word under this umbrella truth: the listener may
never know what is being hypnotically communicated.
They must only reap the benefits of being navigated subconsciously to the best decision.

How Else This Hypnotic Language Pattern Might Be Utilized Applicably In Other Useful Contexts

The benefits of all these language pattern span far deeper than simple conversations. Utilizing these covert indirect techniques provide a head-start for all communications—both verbal and written. For example, you can use these techniques when dealing with customer service representatives to ensure the outcome benefits your desires/objectives. When dealing with teachers and other persons in authority, speaking with this knowledge will navigate conversations and influence their choices for the betterment of yourself. Keep in mind, most people do not know anything whatsoever about hypnotic language—but you do!

Final Purport

In these previous chapters I have shared with you at least twenty-five astonishing hypnotic language patterns. I explained, in this chapter, how they would help you navigate conversations to accomplish specific goals/objectives as well as solidify your foundation to help you learn other hypnotic language pattern techniques. I then shared with you 'why' you should commit to learning and using this hypnotic language pattern; emphasizing the true importance of these linguistic endeavors and techniques in terms of influencing others through hypnotic language. Then I shared everything you needed to know about the hypnotic language patterns; namely: (a) all listeners are unaware of your techniques, (b) respecting free will while simultaneously influencing your subject's hypnotic mind can create win-win outcomes, and (c) how to maintain this technique while using other language patterns. After explaining what you needed to know, I explained step-by-step 'how' you can use these hypnotic language patterns to achieve any result you desire. Explicitly, I told you that step one meant doing and saying specific words with the understanding the listener in unaware of your actions; that step two you should maintain the goal of using suggestive words while simultaneously playing to the listeners subconscious, and step three you must integrate other hypnotic language pattern techniques with other hypnotic techniques (e.g., voice control and alteration, tonal marking and analogue marking embedded commands, etc.). Lastly, we explored some other ways hypnotic language patterns might be useful. We took an interdisciplinary approach and decided hypnotic language patterns could be used in other context: as in customer service interactions, and when dealing with authority figures. Used in these contexts the benefits one might realize could include: (a) accomplishing goals in regards to customer service issues, (b) avoid harsher-than-necessary punishments from authority figures, and (c) navigating all conversations with respect while building greater and greater rapport with your subject(s).

After Thought

Now that you know how to hypnotize people with your words, it's probably best to continue your learning. One way I recommend you go about this is to visit my website: www.indirectknowledge.com and learn from the thousands upon thousands of blog posts I have written on this subject matter.

Why you might want to entertain this idea is because I've done all the leg-work for you. I've taken years of my life, spent hundreds of thousands of dollars (probably closer to a million dollars) researching and learning this subject from some of the world's best hypnotists and sales professionals. There's also always something interesting which will engage your attention and help you to improve on your influence and persuasion skills.

What you might also decide to do is, buy some more of my books and training aids. These aids have been meticulously architected to ensure that you learn fast, and at the highest level you can. The materials I offer up for sale are well below the prices that many other trainers offer up their products at. This means you'll not only save money, but learn, more likely, at a higher level.

How you can go about strategizing the techniques you've learnt here is to continue learning more hypnotic language patterns, committing them to memory, and both creating imaginary scenarios in your mind of you using the patterns, while also taking the time to practice them on real people in real scenarios. I've found that I learned the hypnotic language patterns quicker when I role-played out scenarios in my mind, and then practiced them on real live people.

There are many things to gain from all the zillions of insights you'll likely encounter being a student of conversational hypnosis: (a) you'll find new ways of using the patterns to gain massive results you're seeking, (b) you'll discover alternative hybrids to the patterns, by connecting presuppositions with awareness predicates, and so on, (c) you'll start speaking hypnotically without realizing you're speaking hypnotically through unconscious learning, and (d) you'll magnify your results as you toy around with language and become more aware of how other great persuaders and hypnotists communicate. Then you'll be in a place to model greatness for ultimate results.

Once your level of mastery increases, you'll not only spit-off hypnotic language patterns without consciously realizing you're doing so; but, you'll start to appreciate how the world and success starts to become your very own playground, where you can create great wealth for yourself, while enjoying all the great things life has to off you.

Learn Well! Live Well!

Bryan Westra
bryan@indirectknowledge.com
www.indirectknowledge.com

ABOUT THE AUTHOR

Bryan Westra is founder of: Indirect Knowledge Limited; a communication training company. For more information about him, and to learn some astonishingly FREE lessons on similar subjects, visit: www.indirectknowledge.com

9780990513216